D0141490

The Educator's Writing Handbook

Diana C. Reep
The University of Akron

Helen M. Sharp

Allyn and Bacon
Boston • London • Toronto • Sydney • Tokyo • Singapore

AUG 2000

ELMHURST COLLEGE LIBRARY

Vice President, Publisher: Humanities: Joseph Opiela
Marketing Manager: Lisa Kimball
Editorial-Production Service: Raeia Maes, Maes Associates
Manufacturing Buyer: Suzanne Lareau
Cover Administrator: Jennifer Hart

Copyright © 1999 by Allyn & Bacon
A Viacom Company
160 Gould Street
Needham Heights, MA 02194

All rights reserved. No part of the material protected by this copyright notice may be reproduced or utilized in any form or by any means, electronic or mechanical, including photocopying, recording, or by any information storage and retrieval system, without written permission from the copyright owner.

Internet: www.abacon.com

Library of Congress Cataloging-in-Publication Data

Reep, Diana C.
    The educator's writing handbook / Diana C. Reep, Helen M. Sharp.
      p.   cm.
    Includes index.
    ISBN 0-205-28519-8
    1. Communication in education—Handbooks, manuals, etc.
    2. English language—Rhetoric—Handbooks, manuals, etc.   3. English
    language—Style—Handbooks, manuals, etc.   I. Sharp, Helen M.
    II. Title.
    LB1033.5.R44   1999
    808'.06—dc21   98-21618
                                                       CIP

Printed in the United States of America

10 9 8 7 6 5 4 3 2 1   03 02 01 00 99 98

For Kim and Trisha
DCR

For my husband, Bill
HMS

Contents

Preface

The Educator's Writing Handbook is a practical and easy-to-use desktop guide for all educators at all levels, from the teacher in an elementary school to the district superintendent. Students in university educational administration courses also will find this handbook a useful guide to the kinds of writing they will be doing as professionals.

The eleven chapters contain guidelines and models for the types of written communication that educators deal with most frequently, such as information letters to parents, responses to community complaints, guidance reports, press releases, and newsletters. One chapter provides tips for speaking to various groups; another chapter covers guidelines for effective academic résumés and application letters. Chapters 9, 10, and 11 offer a brief review of grammar, punctuation, and mechanics.

We designed these chapters for the busy educator who wants specific guidance for a particular writing task. For each topic, we explain the purpose of the communication, provide an easy-to-follow checklist for writing the opening, body, and closing of the document, and include a model that illustrates the recommended strategies and style. *The Educator's Writing Handbook* contains 55 models demonstrating effective messages for educational situations.

Sections contain cross references that direct the reader to related entries throughout the handbook. A comprehensive subject index covers terms in the handbook and alternative terms that readers may be familiar with and look for first. Every educator will find this handbook a convenient guide to handling daily communication tasks.

Acknowledgments

Many people contributed in various ways to the development of this handbook. We are grateful for the advice and assistance of the following people: Emily Ann Allen, Excelsior Springs Public Schools, Missouri; Gerald J. Alred, University of Wisconsin–Milwaukee; Richard Angel, Unity Point School, Illinois; Sandra Baker, Carbondale, Illinois; Faye Dambrot, University of Akron, Ohio; Trisha Dean, G. Douglas Donoho, and Sharon Norlander, Buffalo Grove High School, Illinois; John Dively and Shirley Miles-Gename, Carbondale Community High School–Central Campus, Illinois; Patricia George, formerly with the National Association of Secondary School Principals Publications; John R. Harland, Marion High School, Illinois; Ronald G. Harley and Marlene Harley, Oak Forest, Illinois; Paul Kren, Illinois State Board of Education; Michael Perkins, Southern Illinois University; Eugenia Cooper Potter, *NASSP Bulletin* editor; Joann Robb, Director, Grants & Legislative Affairs, Akron Public Schools, Ohio; Karen Russell, Ohio State Board of Education; William L. Sharp, Southern Illinois University; Laura Taylor, Indiana Department of Education; James K. Walter, Texas A&M University at Corpus Christi; William Weber, Libertyville High School, Illinois; Susie Webster, Noblesville, Indiana; and Steve Webster, former school board member, Noblesville, Indiana. We also thank the reviewers of the manuscript: Kathleen Fite, Southwest Texas State University, and John Zelazek, Central Missouri State University.

At Allyn and Bacon, Joseph Opiela led this project from the initial idea through to completion; Rebecca Ritchie provided valuable editorial assistance. Finally, our deep gratitude to Sonia Dial, who cheerfully typed, retyped, sorted, and copied multiple drafts of every page.

D. C. R.
H. M. S.

Introduction

Educators must communicate frequently with various groups and individuals about education issues. Consider this typical school day. The district superintendent writes a report to the school board about budgetary changes. The sixth-grade teacher writes a letter to parents, reminding them about the upcoming science fair. The high school principal writes a memo to faculty and staff explaining new security arrangements. The high school chemistry teacher writes a recommendation letter for a student. The assistant superintendent writes a grant proposal seeking funds to enhance computer classrooms. The high school counselor writes a report about a student. Whatever position an educator holds, successful communication is an important part of the job.

As *accountability* has become the key term in education, school personnel must deliver education-related information to various groups and individuals about such issues as academic standards, state testing programs, block scheduling, school finance equity, and disciplinary policies. If readers understand these school issues and the district's programs, they probably will support the schools. No one can deliver information about education more effectively than school personnel who are experts on the issues and who know their students and school communities. Often, however, educators find themselves frustrated by writing tasks, confused about organizing information and ideas, uncertain how to begin a document, and hesitant about what to include.

WRITING AT WORK

Relying on instinct will not automatically produce clear, effective documents. Writing is a skill requiring the application of communication principles and strategies. Educators writing on the job face two major drawbacks.

No formal training—Educators generally have little specific training in writing the kinds of documents needed in their work. Usually, the first-year college composition course, which covers writing essays, represents the most recent formal instruction in writing techniques. Administrators and teachers take courses in subject matter, educational theory, and administrative principles, but not in professional writing skills.

Too little time—Days are filled with multiple responsibilities, leaving little time for careful writing. Teachers have classes, student conferences, and duty assignments. Administrators face meetings with school boards, community groups, faculty, and staff, and they must deal with disciplinary issues, media questions, and government agencies.

COMMUNICATION PRESSURES ON EDUCATORS

School districts and educators, already under great pressure to expand efficient learning opportunities for students, must communicate with diverse audiences. These readers vary in their understanding of and interest in contemporary school issues. Consider these examples of audiences with which educators must communicate:

- State legislators checking compliance with academic mandates
- Parents concerned about school security
- Teachers adapting to new curriculum guidelines
- Media reporters focusing on student testing and test scores
- Business owners complaining about recent graduates' basic skills
- Students requesting changes in regulations and procedures
- Special-interest groups advocating their positions on such issues as sex education, creationism, multiculturalism, or values education
- Taxpayers upset over district requests for increased funding

These readers have differing opinions and interests and also may not understand specialized educational terms. Writing an effective message about complex educational issues to such diverse readers requires careful attention to selecting appropriate information, explaining specialized terms, and organizing a document, so readers can understand and use the information effectively.

BENEFITS FROM CLEAR COMMUNICATION

Jumbled and confusing messages create anger, confusion, and distrust in readers. Conflicts over issues then escalate. Specific benefits come from writing clear, organized documents.

- Relationships between educators and readers improve because everyone understands the facts of a situation.
- Educators have the opportunity to emphasize the challenges confronting school systems and explain priorities to readers who previously were uninformed about educational issues.
- Educators can highlight school successes and counter vague insinuations of failures.
- Educators will clarify their own thinking about an issue as they explain it to a reader, and writing often stimulates new ideas about a topic.

Educators should look on every opportunity to write as an opportunity to reach interested groups and individuals with pertinent information and to increase their understanding and appreciation of school policies, programs, and services.

This handbook is a practical, "nuts and bolts" guide for educators who must produce effective documents and presentations directed to a specific audience for a specific purpose.

Avoid Negative Language

Use neutral or positive language where possible.

No: Your son, Todd, is failing algebra.

Yes: Your son, Todd, has a 60 average in algebra.

No: I regret telling you about this problem.

Yes: I believe you should know the facts.

1

The Writer's Process

Effective writers think of the writing process as a series of distinct stages—planning, organizing, drafting, and revising. Most writers, however, do not move through these stages in a straight line. Rather, they rethink their writing decisions as they go along and often return to an earlier stage to revise the content or the organization. While writing, you may get new ideas, have new insights into your purpose, realize something new about your readers, or change your mind about appropriate organization and format. You also will develop a personal writing process to match the conditions under which you write. Some writers like to do a full draft before any revising. Others like to revise as they progress, changing sentences and rearranging paragraphs.

One particular system will not be appropriate for all writers, but experienced writers focus on the individual stages of the writing process, so they can maintain control over their writing tasks amid the interruptions of a normal workday.

A busy educator rarely has blocks of uninterrupted time to write. Instead, writing memos about new procedures and letters about school events has to be incorporated into an already full schedule. If you think of writing as a process with distinct steps, you will be able to begin a writing project, handle an interruption, and return to the project without having to start over.

The three major elements of any writing task are *reader, purpose,* and *situation.* When you write a message, you have a specific purpose for that message. Your readers have special interests and levels of understanding. You must write a document that will provide readers with all the necessary information and help them understand and respond appropriately. The writing situation encompasses your specific reader and purpose, as well as pressures of time, controversy, and priorities. Consider the following example of a school administrator and his writing situations.

ONE PRINCIPAL'S WRITING PROCESS

John Hawthorne, principal of Hollow Hills Middle School, must write an article about the upcoming parent–teacher conferences for the school newsletter to be mailed to the parents of the children enrolled in the school. He knows his readers will be interested in information about times, dates, and teachers' rooms, along with suggestions for discussing their children's progress. Principal Hawthorne wants to use his article not only to provide basic information, but also to persuade the parents to attend the conference nights; therefore, his purpose in writing is both informational and persuasive. Because parent attendance has been low in the past two years, he is afraid his readers may not be interested in his article.

To gain his readers' attention, Hawthorne decides to begin his article with an interesting anecdote about student activities at the start of the new school year. He also includes recent research that indicates parent–teacher conferences have a positive effect on a child's progress and future success in school. His writing situation is restricted by time because he must finish the article before noon, so his secretary can incorporate it into the newsletter and begin the copying and mailing process.

That same day, Principal Hawthorne also has to write a memo to the faculty and staff thanking them for a smooth start to the semester. He knows his readers have been upset during the first two weeks of school because some textbooks did not arrive on time and the parking lot repaving, which was supposed to be finished by midsummer, was still in progress. Faculty and staff have to park three blocks away in a public lot. Therefore, his purpose is not only to thank them for their efforts, but also to assure them that the inconveniences will soon be over.

This writing situation differs from the first because the readers do not have to be persuaded to act. The faculty and staff are unhappy and need an expression of appreciation for their efforts under difficult circumstances. Hawthorne decides to emphasize team spirit in the memo as a way of improving faculty and staff morale. He wants to get the memo in the office mailboxes before the first faculty meeting scheduled for the next afternoon.

Before writing either of these documents, Principal Hawthorne took time to focus on the first stage of the writing process.

PLANNING YOUR WRITING

In the planning stage, you must analyze your reader, purpose, and writing situation. Do not start writing before you have a clear understanding of these three elements.

Analyzing Your Reader

Remember that readers differ in what they know about a subject, how they feel about it, what they want to know, and what they can understand. Before you write, consider these questions about your readers:

- Are my readers professional educators or laypersons?
- How will the readers use this document?
- What information are they interested in?
- What do they already know about the situation?
- Will they understand specialized educational terms?
- Do they have positive or negative attitudes toward the subject, the school, or specific people?
- Are there special features, such as headings, checklists, pie graphs, that will help the readers?

Analyzing Your Purpose

Every message has a purpose. To select the most appropriate style, organization, and format, you must determine what you want to accomplish with your document. The following are typical purposes:

- *To inform*—You supply information and explain data to readers. The readers are interested but do not have to take action based on the information. A letter to parents may describe the school's successful athletic teams and plans for the next season. Readers are interested, but they do not have to take action. A memo to the staff may announce plans for a new school building. When writing to inform readers, include the following:

- Specific details about the subject
- Importance of the subject for the school, students, faculty, or academic programs
- Any significant cause and effect relationships

- *To aid decision making*—You supply information and analyze the data so that the reader can make a decision based on the facts. A report to the school board about conditions in the high school gym can aid the board in making budget decisions. A report about suspected gang activity can be used in developing new security systems for a district's schools. When the readers must make decisions based on your documents, include the following:

  - All relevant facts that affect the situation
  - Specific alternatives suggested by people with special knowledge or authority
  - Importance of the decision relative to the school's goals and mission
  - Significant deadlines
  - Breakdown of information into topics or stages relevant to the situation
  - Actions already taken and resulting progress or changes

- *To instruct*—You explain to readers how they should perform a procedure and why it is needed. Readers may be students, parents, faculty, staff, school board members, or administrators. Letters to parents explaining the procedures for signing children up for extracurricular activities, memos to the staff outlining new enrollment procedures, and memos to faculty explaining how to fill out the new attendance forms are all documents that instruct. When writing to instruct, include the following:

  - Purpose of the procedures
  - Each necessary step in the procedures
  - Special conditions that could affect the procedures

- *To record*—You write a document describing specific details about an event, a decision, student progress, or a personnel matter. The primary purpose of the document is to record information for readers in the future. Minutes of a school board meeting, guidance counselor reports about students, and file memos describing policy discussions are all documents whose main purpose is to be a permanent record. Include the following:

    - Reference to relevant background
    - Past history of this issue
    - Decisions or suggested alternatives
    - Assigned responsibilities
    - Events and their consequences
    - Results of tests, surveys, and experiments

- *To persuade*—You urge the readers to take specific actions or reach specific conclusions about an issue. To persuade your readers, you must convince them that the situation requires action, the subject is important, your information is relevant, and it supports your position. A letter to community members asking for volunteers to serve on a school policy committee, a request to the school board for increased funding, a recommendation report suggesting a change in policy are all persuasive documents. To persuade readers to accept your position on a subject, you should include the following:

    - How the subject affects students, school policies, programs, or school atmosphere
    - Importance or urgency of the situation
    - Reasons for your recommendation
    - Reasons why an alternative is not acceptable
    - Expected benefits
    - Negative consequences if your position is not supported

- *To interest*—You present information to satisfy a reader's curiosity. The long-range benefit of writing to interest a reader may be future support with a difficult issue or funding. Most school newsletters have interest as their main purpose. When writing to increase the reader's interest in school matters, include the following:

    - How and why the subject affects students or school atmosphere
    - Amusing, appealing, or startling news or anecdotes
    - Practical effects of complex decisions

Analyzing Your Writing Situation

You probably will be aware of deadlines that may affect how much you can write in a given situation. Consider also the atmosphere in which you are writing. The following elements will affect how and what you write:

- The authority you and your readers have in the school organization and the particular situation
- Traditional preferences for certain kinds of documents, formats, or styles in certain situations
- The school's established relationship with community members, school board, local media, faculty, staff, and students
- Governmental regulations and agency interactions
- Ethical codes and school mission
- Controversy or emotional climate of the subject

Evaluate your reader, purpose, and writing situation before you begin writing, so you can create a document that will be an effective tool in accomplishing the work of your organization.

ORGANIZING YOUR WRITING

The organization stage requires considerable attention because a badly organized document confuses and frustrates readers. In addition, you are writing as an educator, and, if your document is disorganized, readers are likely to think the educational program offered at your school is also disorganized.

The organization stage of writing involves gathering information, grouping major topics, selecting an appropriate organization pattern, and outlining the document structure. This stage is particularly important for maintaining control over your writing. If you are interrupted while writing, you will be able to return to your document and continue without having to re-create your earlier decisions about organization and content.

Gathering Information

You probably will have most of the information about the writing topic before you begin. After evaluating your reader and purpose, you may need to gather more data or clarify facts. Cutting material from the final draft because you have too much information is always easier than padding at the last moment because you have too little. Your document should be the following:

- Accurate
- Up to date
- Relevant to the subject
- Aimed at the reader's understanding

In any situation, delay writing and check the facts rather than include vague or inaccurate information.

Grouping Major Topics

When you have all necessary information, you need to identify the major topics and arrange the information within each topic. Consider these questions:

- Does the subject have obvious divisions? Readers waiting for a report on a high school's athletic program may be interested in salaries, coaches' backgrounds, and student participation. Those then become the major topics.
- Does the reader of this document prefer information grouped under certain topics? If the superintendent likes to see a specific section devoted to technology in every budget request, provide it.
- Which specific major topics will help the reader use the information effectively? If the principal is writing a memo about new supervisory assignments, grouping them according to location, such as hall duty, cafeteria duty, or playground duty, may be most useful for the readers.

Identifying Subtopics

After you determine the major topics in your document, consider the best internal order for the information. Do not clump all the information for a topic under the heading without developing a logical internal structure. Consider these questions:

- What organization for this information will help readers understand most easily? If you have a large report section headed "Costs," sorting the data into subtopics of "Faculty/Staff Salaries," "Maintenance Costs," and "New Materials/Equipment Costs" should help readers understand the differences among these categories.

- Which order will help readers use this document effectively? If you are explaining priorities to the staff, begin with the most important priority and arrange the others in descending order of importance. Readers can then concentrate on specific goals in the order that you have decided is best.
- Which order will have a persuasive effect? If you are persuading readers to take action or to accept a position on an issue, first describe the problem that needs to be solved and then describe the potential solution. Readers are more likely to resist change or new ideas if they do not have a clear understanding of the situation that is prompting change.

Selecting Appropriate Organization Patterns

Research in communication indicates that certain specific organization patterns work best in certain situations. Along with decisions about major topics and internal organization, you should consider the type of message you are sending. Letters announcing good news should be organized differently from letters announcing bad news because readers respond differently to these messages. Also, over time, readers have come to expect specific organization patterns for particular types of messages. Press releases begin with a paragraph that covers the five Ws—who, what, where, when, why; proposals have a budget section. Long-established organization patterns are templates for you to consider while planning your document.

As a writer, you always make choices in content and organization based on your evaluation of your reader, purpose, and writing situation. To help you, the chapters in this handbook present organization patterns for typical documents written by educators.

Outlining the Document Structure

Busy professionals seldom have time to make a formal outline of a document, but most efficient writers compose a master list of topics and subtopics in the order that seems most effective before writing. A master list is a map showing you where specific information will appear in your document. The list will help you control your writing and speed up the writing task.

- You can keep track of your decisions about organization and content in spite of unavoidable interruptions.
- You can concentrate on clearly presenting your information in your first draft, instead of organizing and writing at the same time.
- Knowing the overall structure of your document as you write helps clarify what you want to say.

WRITING YOUR DRAFT

With careful planning and organizing, your first draft, in the case of short memos or letters, could be your final draft. Long reports or letters on sensitive subjects probably require several drafts. When you begin writing, focus on explaining the information you have gathered and organized, and do not worry about grammar and punctuation or fine points of style. Pausing to look up the rules for capitalization will interfere with your covering the subtopics thoroughly.

Follow your master list of topics and write quickly. When you have covered every item on your list, you have a full draft of your document.

REVISING YOUR DOCUMENT

Most writers do some revising as they progress through these writing stages because new ideas occur about content and organization. However, once you have a full draft, it is time to look at it carefully for ways to improve it. Unless the document is very short, you will want to revise in two stages: overall structure and sentence level editing.

Revising Overall Structure

Evaluate once more your reader and purpose, and then review your choice of format. Consider whether changes are necessary in the following areas.

- *Content*—Have you included enough details and facts to enable your readers to understand your message and respond appropriately?
- *Definitions*—Do you need to define terms for lay readers?
- *Major topics*—Have you identified the topics most helpful and familiar to your readers? Does the internal organization suit the needs of the readers?

- *Headings*—Do you have descriptive headings that will guide your readers to the information they need?
- *Openings and closings*—Does your opening establish the subject and tell readers the overall purpose of the document? Does your closing summarize the major facts, include necessary recommendations, or suggest future action? Do your readers need to be told what to do next?
- *Visuals*—Do you need to include maps, photographs, drawings, or charts and tables to aid reader understanding?

Editing on the Sentence Level

After making any changes in the overall organization and appearance of your document, edit for grammar, punctuation, and mechanics. Chapters 9, 10, and 11 discuss these elements and provide guidance for revision.

Do not rush the revision process, especially for documents dealing with sensitive issues or priorities. Many writers try to leave time (several hours or overnight) between finishing the draft and revising. This break allows you to disengage from the subject and your writing while you concentrate on a new task. Then, when you return to your document, you should be able to see ways to improve it.

Educators at all levels face daily hectic schedules, and the pressure to write clear, effective documents for various purposes adds to the tension of the workday. However, you can manage important writing tasks by following the steps of the writing process—planning, organizing, drafting, and revising. You can control your written communication from the first idea to the final document.

Become familiar with the steps in the writing process and incorporate them into your own writing tasks. You will notice improved efficiency in writing school documents. Review this chapter and the other sections of this handbook for reminders about effective strategies for writing and models of types of messages.

Use Concrete Terms

many students . . . . two-thirds of the students

improved effort. . . . . completed all homework

disruptive . . . . shouts out during class

as soon as possible . . . . by Friday, May 16

2

Correspondence

Correspondence includes both letters and memos addressed to one person or to a group. Although you may address your correspondence to a particular person, that person may pass on your letter or memo to others. Because correspondence emphasizes communication between individuals, it can elicit an emotional response in the reader, and sensitive issues must be carefully handled to avoid misunderstandings. Parents might respond one way to dress code regulations in the student handbook and another way to a letter about a dress code from the principal. In writing correspondence, consider the emotional responses of readers as well as their practical responses to your message.

Letters are written primarily to people who are not members of the school district. Memos are written primarily to people who are members of the school district. In some schools or districts, however, custom may dictate a particular format for certain kinds of messages, such as commendations always being announced in letters.

No matter what the format, consider the tone you are setting in your correspondence and anticipate how readers may react emotionally to your message. *Tone* refers to the feelings and attitude created in your readers by your word choice. Words on paper cannot be cushioned by a smile or a friendly gesture, so choose words that create a pleasant, cooperative tone.

CONSIDERING YOUR READER

No matter what the purpose of your correspondence, think of the subject from your reader's point of view, a strategy called the *you-attitude*. In letters and memos, concentrate on conveying an understanding of your reader's situation and interests. Usually, simple revision of sentences will emphasize the reader's point of view. Here are guidelines for creating the you-attitude in your correspondence:

- Look at a situation from the reader's perspective and emphasize his or her participation.

  No: We are all pleased with Gary's success in passing the standardized tests.

  Yes: Gary put forth the extra effort needed to successfully complete the standardized tests.

- Emphasize the reader's benefits in a situation.

  No: The new cafeteria regulations have made the school day easier for our teachers.

  Yes: The new cafeteria regulations have created a pleasant, safe atmosphere for your children.

- Offer an appreciative comment whenever possible.

  No: We have exceeded last year's fund raising total to purchase band equipment.

  Yes: Thanks to your efforts, nearly $5,000 has been added to our fund total for band equipment.

- Avoid words that sound accusing or insulting.

  No: You failed to turn in your lesson plans for last week

  Yes: Please turn in last week's lesson plans so your file will be up to date.

- Avoid stressing your feelings; emphasize the reader's achievements or concerns.

  No: I was pleased to hear that your proposal was awarded the Pickens Educational Grant.

  Yes: Congratulations on receiving the Pickens Educational Grant.

By stressing your reader's point of view and benefits in a situation, you can create a friendly, helpful tone in your correspondence and enhance the communication atmosphere inside or outside your organization.

MAINTAINING POSITIVE TONE

The general tone of correspondence is improved if you stress positive rather than negative images. Avoid writing when you are angry or before you have had time to consider all aspects of a troubling situation. If positive words do not seem possible in the circumstances, select neutral words that do not emphasize the negative. Consider the following sentence revisions from a negative emphasis to a positive or neutral one:

Negative: I received your complaint.
Positive: I appreciate hearing about your concerns.
Negative: To avoid further confusion during fire drills, give your students instructions they can understand.
Positive: To be sure students can safely exit the building during fire drills, please tell them which exit to use.
Negative: Your note claimed that Tim had a doctor's appointment.
Neutral: Your note said that Tim had a doctor's appointment.
Negative: I regret to inform you that your request for an aide has been denied.
Neutral: At this time, the budget lacks funds for another aide.

The substitution of only a few words in these sample sentences improves the tone without changing the content of the sentence. Negative language in correspondence decreases cooperation and understanding in readers. Emphasize a positive tone and seek solutions without dwelling on problems.

USING NATURAL LANGUAGE

A further strategy for building an effective tone in letters and memos is to use natural, conversational language. Avoid falling into the habit of using old-fashioned phrases that sound stilted or cold. Readers who have to mentally translate such writing into normal-sounding language get annoyed with both the message and the writer. Artificial language does not impress readers. Create goodwill by sounding natural and interested in the subject. Here are revisions from overly formal language into natural conversational language:

No: Attached hereto is the student progress report about which you inquired.

Yes: Attached is the student progress report you requested.

No: It has come to my attention announcements relative to the annual Spring Talent Show have not been disseminated to appropriate media outlets.

Yes: I understand that announcements about the annual Spring Talent Show need to be sent to the local newspapers and television stations.

No: Kindly be advised that permission for your son or daughter is required on the form enclosed herewith.

Yes: Signing the enclosed form allows your son or daughter to attend the program at the Sandrunne Art Museum.

All professions have jargon—specialized terms only understood by those in the field. Avoid using educational jargon in letters or memos to people who are not educators. Also avoid using jargon that is unique to your school in correspondence to educators at other institutions. Jargon allows people who work together to exchange brief messages, but it often interferes with clarity in regular correspondence. Notice the following revision to eliminate jargon:

No: School District #102 encourages site-based management with stakeholder collaboration.

Yes: School District #102 encourages governance by those in the schools, including collaboration with the school community at large.

ORGANIZING CORRESPONDENCE

Correspondence usually is most effective organized in either a *direct pattern* or an *indirect pattern,* depending on the subject of the message and how the reader is likely to react to the message.

If the message concerns good news or supplies information to readers who are not emotionally affected by the subject, use the direct pattern of organization with the main idea in the opening paragraph. If the message contains bad news for the reader, use the indirect pattern of organization with the main idea stated after an explanation preparing the reader to accept the news. Readers may not read an explanation if it follows the bad news; the indirect pattern is a strategy that presents the bad news in a sensitive manner and tries to create as much goodwill as possible.

A third organization pattern is the *persuasive pattern,* which also delays the main idea until after the explanation or until the closing. Writers use this pattern when readers need to be convinced to act or cooperate.

A letter usually has only one purpose, but a memo to faculty or staff may have several purposes. A memo to high school faculty may be a good news announcement that 90 percent of the seniors have passed the required graduation proficiency test; but if the memo also seeks volunteers for the afternoon tutoring sessions for the remaining 10 percent, the message is also persuasive. Consider each message's purpose to determine the most effective organization strategy.

Good News or Information Messages

Letters and memos that convey good news or provide information in a nonemotional situation use the direct organization pattern. This pattern fits most correspondence situations. Models 2-1 and 2-2 illustrate this pattern. The direct pattern has three distinct sections:

Opening

- Identify the main subject of the message.
- State the purpose of the letter or memo.
- Identify any correspondence you are answering.

Model 2-1, an answer to an inquiry, opens by telling the reader the requested materials are enclosed. The memo in Model 2-2 identifies a problem in the computer center and asks the reader's help in solving it.

Body

- Explain the relevant details about the situation.
- Answer the reader's questions.
- Offer more description, or provide guidance for future action.
- Clarify any procedures or future actions.
- Number questions if you are asking several of them.
- Respond to each question asked in incoming correspondence. If you cannot immediately answer a question, say so in your message.
- Maintain a friendly, helpful tone.
- Identify any benefits to the reader or the school.

MODEL 2–1 Information Letter in Direct Organization Pattern (Semiblock Style)

CATHCART ACADEMY
  WILLOW ROAD & HIGHWAY 14
   RIVER HILLS, WI 53028
   (414-555-8844)

September 28, 1999

Ms. Laura F. Hayward
332 W. Forest Drive
River Hills, WI 53029

Dear Ms. Hayward:

I am happy to provide information about our program for children with special needs. As you requested in your letter of September 22, 1999, I am enclosing our brochure explaining our program for children with communicative disorders. Also enclosed is the description of Cathcart Academy's teaching methods and courses and brief biographies of our faculty, all with special training to support our program.

Cathcart Academy was established in 1924 as the Branwell School by the Branwell Foundation for the Hearing Impaired, but the academy became an independent school in 1948 with a variety of programs individualizing kindergarten through sixth grade instruction. Many parents prefer to explore the services of our specialized school before sending their children to an institution that mainstreams all students.

I'm sure you have many questions about the educational programs we offer and how your child can benefit from them. If you would like to tour our facilities, I will be happy to show you the adapted classrooms and our Speech and Hearing Center. Please call me at 555–8844 between 8:00 a.m. and 5:00 p.m. to discuss your child's needs or to make an appointment for a tour.

Sincerely,

Katherine L. Gault

Katherine L. Gault
Executive Director

KLG:sd
Enc. (2)

MODEL 2–2   Information Memo in Direct Organization Pattern

To: Faculty and Staff

From: Mark Kowalski   *Mark*
               Computer Center Manager

Date: October 3, 1999

Re: Screensavers

We have encountered a problem in the Computer Center and need your help to solve it. Julie DeCastro reported yesterday afternoon that, when her sophomore English students turned on their computers, sexually explicit screensavers appeared. I checked every computer in the Center this morning and eliminated these screensavers, but whoever installed them may strike again.

Please report to me immediately if inappropriate material appears on the computers your class is using. Also, please make a note of the time, date, and which computers were involved and give me a brief description of the material when you report a problem. I will eliminate the offensive material and share the information with Principal Hendrix. We are trying to discover who is responsible for the screensavers that appeared yesterday.

Although this incident may have been meant as a joke, we are treating the situation as a serious misdemeanor as it involves offensive material that may qualify as sexual harassment. Please see me if you have any information that will help us clear up the situation.

Model 2-1 provides some background about the school and explains why parents find the school useful. The middle paragraph in Model 2-2 gives the readers directions about what to do if they encounter the computer problem.

Closing

- Remind the reader about any deadlines.
- Call for action by the reader.
- Reaffirm the importance or urgency of the subject.
- Ask for the reader's cooperation.

Model 2-1 suggests the reader's next action; Model 2-2 explains why this problem is important.

The direct organization plan gets the communication off to a clear start, quickly provides information, and ends by directing the reader to the next stage if necessary.

Bad News Messages

Correspondence that conveys bad news is best presented in the indirect organization pattern. When you write negative messages, you can presume your readers will be upset or become angry at learning the bad news. Avoid putting the bad news in the opening paragraph (called a *buffer* paragraph) or in a subject line because readers are likely to ignore your explanations and concentrate on their own negative feelings. Models 2-3 and 2-4 illustrate the indirect pattern to convey bad news. Following are the elements in the indirect pattern:

Opening

- Establish a friendly, concerned tone.
- Avoid any direct mention of the main subject or the negative news.
- Do not use negative words or references to the bad news.
- Agree with the reader about a general situation.
    You are right when you say that...
- State your awareness of the importance of the person or organization.
    Your organization has been a long-standing...
- State good news if there is any.
    I am happy to send one of the reports you asked for.
- Express a sincere compliment.
    Your work with the Red Cross has been outstanding.
- Assure the reader you have considered his or her request or situation thoroughly.
    I immediately looked into the situation you described.

Notice that the buffer paragraph in Model 2-3 shows an appreciation of the past work of the organization. In Model 2-4, the buffer paragraph contains genuine praise for the work of the reader.

Body

- Explain the circumstances of the situation.
- Assure the reader of careful attention to the matter.

**MODEL 2–3   Bad News Letter in Indirect Organization Pattern
(Full-Block Style)**

ST. CATHERINE'S ELEMENTARY SCHOOL
1200 N. Ridgemont Street
Cleveland Heights, OH 44122
(216–555–2341)

November 12, 1999

Mrs. Kimberly Everett
President
Hillsdale Garden Club
4122 Surrey Lane
Cleveland Heights, OH 44122

Dear Mrs. Everett:

I am a personal supporter of the Hillsdale Garden Club because my
mother was one of the founding members and helped institute the
annual charity sale that benefits the children's playgrounds in
Cleveland Heights.

When I received your request to use our grounds for your annual
sale, May 15–17, 2000, I immediately consulted our governing
board. One of St. Catherine's long-standing policies is to cooperate
with community groups in an equitable manner. Because we believe
the school grounds are part of the school proper, we have never
allowed outside organizations to use the grounds no matter how
worthy the purpose. Our governing board reaffirmed this earlier
decision when considering your request.

Although St. Catherine's cannot assist you in planning your annual
sale, I recommend that you call Jeffrey Voight (555-6767), Director
of the Sleepy Hollow Senior Home. The grounds are large enough for
your annual sale, and the seniors living there probably would enjoy
the beautiful display your sale creates. Best wishes for your group's
activities in the coming year.

Sincerely,

Marjorie P. Kurtiz

Marjorie P. Kurtiz
Principal

MPK:rt

MODEL 2–4   Bad News Memo in Indirect Organization Pattern

MANSFIELD PARK HIGH SCHOOL

MEMORANDUM

To: Leslie Timkins

From: Randall Washington *RW*
               Assistant Principal

Date: February 6, 1999

Re: Travel Request

Leslie, your work with the statewide Science Initiative Project has been outstanding. Both Principal Carson and I believe the second place award won by your senior chemistry class at the 1998 Science Forum is a direct result of your concentrated efforts in developing an impressive project and display.

When we budgeted conference travel funds for 1998–1999, we covered the state conference on secondary school departmental reorganization and also funded the music educators' conference in Tacoma, Washington. The priority for music education stems from our band, which is developing into a fine representative at competitions. We did not anticipate the extraordinary efforts you put into the Science Forum. Your interest in attending the Regional Science Teachers' Conference in Jefferson City is understandable; however, we do not have sufficient travel funds this year to cover an additional conference.

Because our participation in the Science Initiative Project is important to our school and in appreciation of your effort, Principal Carson has put your attendance at the conference at the top of the list for travel funds for next year.

- Include significant facts that affect the situation.
- Make the reader aware of specific reasons why the bad news is necessary.

Model 2-3 stresses the decision-making process; Model 2-4 explains the budgetary facts.

Bad News

- Place the bad news immediately after the explanation and in the same paragraph.
- Do not emphasize the negative news or decision by starting the next paragraph with a negative statement.
- Use neutral words if possible, as in Models 2-3 and 2-4.

Closing

- Maintain a pleasant tone.
- If possible, suggest an alternative or indicate a possible favorable decision in the future.

Model 2-3 suggests another location to the reader, and Model 2-4 promises consideration in the next year's budget.

You cannot always give your readers what they want. Use the indirect pattern to help your readers understand the reasons for bad news and avoid harsh announcements that will anger readers.

Persuasive Messages

Correspondence that persuades readers to cooperate and take action in a situation often uses a persuasive indirect pattern designed to appeal to readers' interests. Follow these guidelines:

Opening

- Catch the reader's attention by introducing the subject based on the reader's interests.
- Mention a common interest in solving a problem or creating a mutual benefit.
- Mention startling facts or an intriguing development.

Models 2-5 and 2-6 open with an appeal to a mutual interest: increasing parent–teacher communication in Model 2-5 and improving the public image of the school in Model 2-6.

Body

- Increase the reader's interest in the subject by explaining more details and build the reader's interest in the expected results.

MODEL 2–5   Persuasive Letter

KING CENTER ELEMENTARY SCHOOL
667 South Wilson Drive
Dallas, TX 75205

October 2, 1999

Dear Parents/Guardians:

As a new teacher at King Center Elementary School, I am interested in getting to know the parents/guardians of my students. One way my students share their ideas with me is through "dialogue notebooks." These are notebooks in which the students and I write to each other about any topics that interest them. I believe dialogue notebooks also would be a good way for me to communicate with my students' parents/guardians, particularly those of you who find it difficult to attend the regular conference sessions.

I will send the dialogue notebooks home with your child on Monday, October 6. You will notice that I have written a brief message to you on the first page about the progress your child is making in school or about his or her interests. You may answer my remarks, or you may write on a new topic or ask questions in the notebooks. Send the notebook back to school with your child when you have written a message to me. You do not have to write regularly or on schedule. The notebook provides a way to communicate easily about your child's progress or activities.

These informal conversations are a way to share our interest in your child's progress. I look forward to seeing your messages.

Sincerely,

Tricia Kallen

Tricia Kallen
Fourth Grade Teacher

- Use you-attitude in explaining the benefits of your request or the importance of the situation.

Model 2-5 explains how the writer plans to use the dialogue notebooks to improve parent–teacher communication. In Model 2-6, the writer explains possible areas for teacher participation in the television taping.

MODEL 2–6 Persuasive Memo

To: Faculty and Staff

From: Anne Anderson *AA*
               Assistant Principal

Date: October 10, 1999

Subject: TV Publicity

An interesting way to gain public interest and goodwill for our school
has developed. Channel 6, WKYP, is planning to produce "A Day in
the Life" of a local high school. Several high schools will appear in
the opening segment, but Adams High School has been invited to
participate as the featured school. This television coverage could be
significant in raising public interest in the spring school bond issue
and offers us a way to show off our faculty and students.

The television taping will be done during the school day and take
three days. Disruption should be minimal because all the taping will
be scheduled with the teacher or coach ahead of time. Following are
the areas the television station is interested in taping:

    Classes in the Computer Center
    Practice sessions with the football team
    Science classes conducting laboratory experiments
    Meetings of student clubs
    Cheerleader and pom-pom practices
    Band practice

Taping could include other activities as well. Please consider
volunteering to participate in this taping and help us put Adams in
the forefront of institutions that deserve increased support from the
community. We will distribute parental permission forms later.

Right now, let's all step forward and volunteer to create a dynamic,
positive image of Adams for the local television audience. See Mary
Beth in the office to reserve specific class periods that show student-
centered learning at all levels.

Closing

• Ask for action or repeat the earlier request.
• If the reader must take action, clarify what he or she needs to do.

The closing in Model 2-5 implies that readers will cooperate and return the notebooks with messages. The Model 2-6 closing emphasizes team spirit and directs readers to a particular person to volunteer.

FORMAT

Both letters and memos have traditional formats that readers expect and that help them read the messages quickly.

Letters

The two most common letter formats are illustrated in Model 2-1 (semi-block style) and Model 2-3 (full-block style). In the semiblock style, the date, close, and signature block are just to the right of the center of the page. In the full-block style, which has become the preferred style in most institutions, every line begins at the left margin.

- *Date line*—Most school stationery includes the school name, address, and telephone number. Place the date of the letter two lines below the school letterhead.
- *Inside address*—Place the reader's full name, title, and address two to eight lines below the date at the left margin. Vary the spacing so the letter is centered attractively on the page. Spell out words such as *street, avenue,* and *boulevard,* as well as the city name. Use the U.S. Postal Service two-letter abbreviation for the state with no period. Allow one space between the state and the ZIP code.
- *Salutation*—The salutation appears two lines below the inside address at the left margin. The salutation is always followed by a colon. For formal correspondence, address men as Mr. and women as Ms., unless you know that a woman prefers and uses Mrs. Do not assume that the mother of a student is married. Professional titles, such as Dr., are also appropriate. If you are not sure exactly who your reader is, use the following strategies:

    When writing to a group, use a descriptive title.

    Dear Members of MADD:

    When writing to an institutional position, use an attention line.

    Attention: Director of Research

When writing to someone you cannot identify as a man or woman, use an attention line.

Attention: D. B. Thacker

The attention line appears in place of the salutation at the left margin. Do not use general salutations, such as "Dear Sir" or "Gentlemen," because these may imply a sexist attitude.

- *Subject lines*—Some writers prefer to use a subject line in a letter to identify the main topic. The subject line may appear two lines under the date:

December 12, 1999

Subject: Report Cards

The subject line may also appear two lines below the salutation and two lines above the first line of the letter:

Dear Mrs. Robertson:

Subject: Cromwell High School Open House

We are happy to announce....

Some writers prefer to center the subject line between the salutation and the first line of the letter:

Dear Mrs. Robertson:

Subject: CROMWELL HIGH SCHOOL OPEN HOUSE

We are happy to announce....

The subject line may be underlined or typed in all capitals so readers can see it easily. Never put any negative news in a subject line to any reader.
- *Body*—The body of a letter is single-spaced and double-spaced between paragraphs. Do not justify the right margins because the text will have awkward white spaces between some words, and readers may assume that justified right margins indicate a mass mailing.
- *Close*—The close appears two lines below the last sentence of the letter and consists of a standard expression. The most common closing expression is "Sincerely" or "Sincerely yours." The first word is cap-

italized, but the second is not. The close is always followed by a comma.

- *Signature block*—The signature block is four lines below the close and consists of the writer's name and title. The writer's signature appears in the four-line space between the close and the typed name.
- *Notations*—Notations begin two lines below the signature block at the left margin. In Model 2-1, "KLG" indicates the writer, and "sd" indicates the typist. A colon or slash separates the initials. If materials are enclosed with the letter, use either the abbreviation *Enc.* or the word *Enclosure.* In Model 2-1, the writer indicates how many items are enclosed. Some writers prefer to identify the items: "Enclosure: Fact Sheet." If other people receive copies of the letter, indicate that directly under the enclosure notation: "c: R. Ford." If several people receive copies, list them in rank order, the highest first.
- *Second page*—If your letter has a second page, put the name of the addressee, page number, and date across the top of the page:

Mr. John Jones   2   May 6, 1998

or stacked in the upper-left corner:

Mr. John Jones

page 2

May 6, 1998

Memos

Many schools have printed memo forms to ensure a consistent format. If you have no printed form, use the memo format shown in Models 2-2, 2-4, and 2-6. Note the following:

- *The heading* consists of the name of the reader, your name, the date, and the subject line. Use titles and full names. Memos do not have a closing, so you may initial your typed name in the heading or sign your full name there.
- *The subject line* should be brief but clearly indicate a specific subject. Use key words that will attract your reader's attention. Capitalize the major words. Never indicate negative news in a subject line.

E-MAIL

E-mail (electronic mail) allows you to transmit letters, memos, and other documents from one computer to another through computer networks. E-mail has some advantages over traditional letters and memos:

- You can send a message to many people quickly.
- As a team member working on a project, you can exchange information and ideas quickly without frequent meetings or conference calls.
- You can exchange simple questions and answers with someone without playing "telephone tag."
- You can send your message at odd hours because the receiver can collect and answer it at another time.

Cautions

Use e-mail with caution. Because e-mail does not pass through anyone's hands and readers use a password to access messages, people often assume the messages are private. E-mail is not private.

The institution that pays for the computers and the e-mail service has the right to read all e-mail sent from those computers. Some computer systems save all e-mail even after it is deleted, and computer experts can find e-mail in a system up to five years after it has been deleted.

By pressing one key, a receiver can send your e-mail message to dozens or hundreds of people. Hackers can alter your message and send it under your name. People have been fired and sued as a result of e-mail messages. Follow these cautions when sending e-mail:

- Do not send confidential material via e-mail.
- Do not make flip comments, use profanity, or indulge in mimicry even in a message to someone you consider a friend.
- Do not reveal emotions in e-mail that you would not reveal in a letter or memo.
- Do not answer any e-mail on controversial topics without carefully thinking about your answer. Such subjects should be handled in confidential memos or letters.

Style

E-mail style is still evolving, and e-mail systems vary in their capacities for formatting. Here are some general rules for style:

- Keep the e-mail message fairly brief. Many receivers do not like to scroll through a long message, and most people will have to print out a very long message in order to analyze and respond to it.
- Use headings and lists for clarity in a message that is longer than one screen. If you are asking several questions, number them. If you are responding to questions, number your answers in the same order as the questions were asked.
- Use specific subject lines. Vague subject lines, such as "News," do not alert the reader to the topic. People who get a lot of e-mail may skip messages that do not clearly indicate the subject or the urgency of the message.
- Change subject lines when the message content changes. The "reply" function makes it easy to keep using the same subject line, but communication often changes focus, and the subject line should reflect a change in topic.
- Check spelling and grammar before sending an e-mail message. Readers are less forgiving of such errors from educators than they would be from someone else.
- Avoid icons, such as ":)" (a smile), and abbreviations, such as "IMHO" (in my humble opinion). Not all receivers understand them.
- Use your full name. Even though most e-mail headings include the sender's e-mail address, the address often does not include sufficient identification. "Bob" as a signature line can be confusing to someone who knows more than one Bob. As a courtesy, end your message with your full name, mailing address, telephone number, and e-mail address to receivers outside your institution. Use your full name when ending a message sent within your institution.

E-mail to Parents/Guardians

E-mail from school personnel to parents or guardians can be convenient. Follow these guidelines:

- Do not use e-mail for your first contact. Parents prefer a more formal introduction to school personnel. Telephone or write your first message.
- Use e-mail if the parent has provided an e-mail address and specifically asked that you use it. Working parents may prefer to use e-mail.
- Use e-mail if the situation allows a brief, informal answer.

- Do not use e-mail if the situation is a crisis. Many people do not read their e-mail messages every day.

(See also "Guidelines and Models for Special Correspondence," Chapter 3.)

Avoid Gender Bias in Language

Refer to men and women in similar ways

No: Mr. Johnson and Debbie will hand out materials.

Yes: Mr. Johnson and Ms. Collins will hand out materials.

Eliminate general pronouns where possible.

No: The department chair will prepare his evaluations.

Yes: The department chair will prepare evaluations.

3

Guidelines and Models for Special Correspondence

The basic organization patterns for good news or information, bad news, and persuasion covered in Chapter 2 are appropriate for all correspondence, depending on the reader, purpose, and situation.

This chapter contains specific guidelines and models for the types of messages that educators write frequently.

LETTERS

Letters represent formal communication with parents and community members. Effective letters can create a positive relationship with the readers and involve them in the educational efforts of your school and district.

Commendation Letters

A commendation letter is a formal expression of appreciation for a person's voluntary and extraordinary efforts in a project or special circumstances. A commendation letter is not appropriate when someone has been paid for services.

Purpose
Commendation letters are often useful, particularly for other educators, as evidence of service when the receiver requests promotions, special

assignments, or salary increases. Businesses like to have evidence that their employees are involved in community activities, and the commendation letter provides formal documentation of that service. Recipients may wish to frame the letter for their offices or family rooms as a "personal trophy" they achieved through their volunteer work. Because a commendation letter may be read by many people, personal references to your relationship with the receiver or casual remarks are not appropriate.

Organization

Use the direct organization plan for a commendation letter. Always use official stationery with the full name of your institution. Follow these guidelines:

Opening

- Use a formal salutation even if you are on a first-name basis with the receiver.
- Identify the official project or activity for which you are commending the receiver's efforts.
- Write on behalf of others. Although you are writing the letter, you are a representative of the group that benefited from this person's efforts.

Body

- Mention the difficulty of the project, the time-consuming nature of it, any extraordinary problems that had to be overcome, and any details that show the scope of this person's contribution.
- Use several short paragraphs rather than one long paragraph to describe the person's contributions, so specific factors will stand out.
- Identify successful results from the person's effort, such as enhanced student programs, greater understanding of some issue, or specific achievements by individuals.

Closing

- Repeat general appreciation for the person's work and reaffirm that you are writing for others as well as yourself.

Model 3-1 illustrates a commendation letter written by a principal to a professor at a nearby university. The letter identifies the specific project in the opening paragraph and commends the professor's work. Two

MODEL 3–1   Commendation Letter

WHITFIELD HIGH SCHOOL
6900 Ridgewood Road
Whitfield, MO 64933
(813) 555–6878

April 12, 1999

Dr. Robert F. Winston
Associate Professor
Dept. of English
Missouri Central University
University Park, MO 64922

Dear Dr. Winston:

On behalf of Whitfield High School, the faculty, and the students who participated in the Midwest Regional Creative Writing Contest of 1999, I want to commend you for your extraordinary efforts in organizing our students' entries in the poetry and short story divisions and in securing the help of your two colleagues, Dr. Daryl Molini and Ms. Nina Pommer, in judging the initial round.

We all appreciate the time involved in handling this project, which began in November 1998 with counseling students on how to prepare entries and ended when the winners were announced on April 6, 1999. Naturally, we are especially pleased that one of our students, Angela Gomez, placed third in the poetry division. Angela's talents, like those of other Whitfield students who entered the contest, might have remained undeveloped if not for your efforts in working with these beginning writers.

Your work with our students has had a lasting effect in that the first Whitfield Creative Writing Club was formed during the contest process. You have the deepest appreciation of all of us at Whitfield, as well as the parents and students who directly benefited from your efforts.

Sincerely yours,

John N. Westwood

John N. Westwood
Principal

JNW/hr

---

other people also receive recognition here because the professor recruited them. The middle paragraph mentions the length of his commitment, adds details about the creative writing contest, and mentions the student who placed the highest. Notice that the writer connects student achievements to the receiver's volunteer efforts. The closing mentions another positive outcome resulting from the professor's efforts and repeats the general appreciation of all parties. This letter will be useful to the professor if he needs to provide his dean with evidence of community service.

Information Letters to Parents/Guardians

Letters to parents or guardians frequently provide information about school activities and may include some form of instructions for the parents.

Purpose

A letter to parents always involves establishing trust and assuring the parents that their child is involved in a positive educational experience. Anticipate and respond to their concerns about the safety and supervision of any particular activity, and provide precise details about arrangements. Include any instructions necessary for the parents to help the child. Although information is the primary reason for the letter, always think of your message as good public relations for the school.

Organization

Use the direct organization pattern for a letter that provides information. Assume that your readers want a lot of detail. Follow these guidelines:

Opening

- Identify the exact reason for writing in the opening paragraph.
- Use full names for programs, exact identification for sponsoring agencies or companies, precise dates, and locations.
- State the overall purpose of the activity you are writing about.

Body

- Provide detailed descriptions, instructions, and explanations about the expected results or importance of activities and all relevant information that an interested parent would want.

- Sound enthusiastic about the activity if it is a positive one. If you are writing about activities to solve a problem, state your confidence that the problem will be resolved.

Closing

- Explain any action that the parents must take at once. Identify any deadlines for action.
- Offer to answer questions or provide more information.

Models 3-2 and 3-3 show typical information letters to parents. Model 3-2 provides information about homecoming activities, so parents can monitor their children's schedules. Notice that parents are invited to the bonfire and parade. The closing reflects enthusiasm about the event. Model 3-3 introduces a new reading activity and explains the details. The writer asks for parental support for the reading program and offers to discuss it in more detail with interested parents.

(See also "Good News or Information Messages" in Chapter 2.)

Inquiry Letters to Businesses and Services

An inquiry letter is a request for information about a particular program, event, product, service, or person.

Purpose

The inquiry letter should request specific information, so the reader can respond with appropriate facts and details. If the inquiry does not ask focused questions, the reader often does not know how best to answer. Write to a specific person for the information. Avoid addressing inquiry letters to departments or organizations in general because no one will be responsible for answering you.

Organization

Inquiry letters represent routine business. Use the direct organization pattern. Follow these guidelines:

Opening

- State your overall reason for needing information about the subject.
- State your inquiry and indicate you need information in several areas.
- Identify any third party who told you to write, such as, "David Roberts at Shorewood High School suggested I contact you."

MODEL 3–2   Information Letter to Parents/Guardians

SOUTH CENTRAL HIGH SCHOOL
567 Vermont Road
Newton Springs, Vermont 05744
(802) 555–6282

October 1, 1999

Dear Parents/Guardians:

Activities for South Central High's Homecoming Weekend are scheduled for October 12–13. We want this weekend to be both exciting and safe for our students. Following are the scheduled activities for Homecoming Weekend.

Homecoming activities officially begin with a **pep rally** on **Friday, October 12,** at **3:00 p.m.** in Webster Field. All fall sports teams will receive recognition. Coach Simmons will speak about our football past and South Central's traditions. At **7:00 p.m.** at the north end of Webster Field, a **Homecoming Bonfire** will provide a warm welcome to returning alumni. Please join us for the bonfire and cider and snacks in the fieldhouse immediately following the fight song.

Saturday, October 13, begins with the **parade of floats** at **11:30 a.m.** starting on 16th Street and Vermont Road and continuing to the stadium. **Pregame** ceremonies begin at **1:00 p.m.** with a welcome by Mayor Donald Emerson and South Central alumna Bettina Lewis, president of Northeast Engineering Consultants. Awards for alumni outstanding achievements will follow. The Rotary will open **food booths** a half-hour before the **2:30 p.m.** game against the Stanleyville Wolverines.

The **Homecoming Dance** will begin at **8:30 p.m.** in the gymnasium, and Homecoming Queen Lahna Nelson and King Curt Merrick will be crowned midway through the dance.

We are all looking forward to South Central's 1999 Homecoming Weekend, and your participation is welcome. Let's all cheer our Tigers on as they meet the ferocious Wolverines!

Sincerely,

Bradley Curtis

Bradley Curtis
Principal

BC:dc

MODEL 3–3   Information Letter to Parents/Guardians

MARTHA WASHINGTON ELEMENTARY SCHOOL
Atkins Center, Virginia 22858
(703) 555–0027

September 16, 1999

Dear Parents/Guardians:

The fourth-grade class will be participating in the state READING FOR FUN AND KNOWLEDGE program, from October 1 through December 1. The program goal is to motivate beginning readers to read more and develop a positive attitude toward reading as entertainment. Our local sponsor is the El Matador Restaurant. The program is as follows:

1. Your child selects a book from the library-approved collection for the fourth grade.
2. Your child reads the book outside school and fills out a READING FOR FUN AND KNOWLEDGE checklist for the book. Children usually have no trouble filling out the checklist, but you may be asked for help.
3. Your child's checklist is placed in a Personal Reading Folder in my classroom.
4. Children accumulating ten checklists by December 1 will be awarded a STAR READER RIBBON and a coupon for a dinner at the El Matador Restaurant.
5. Children accumulating fifteen or more reading checklists by December 1 will be awarded a STAR READER RIBBON and receive a coupon for a dinner for four at the El Matador Restaurant.

Books from your home may also be used for the program after I check their reading level. With your support, our class will have a successful reading program this fall. Please call me with any questions you may have about READING FOR FUN AND KNOWLEDGE.

Sincerely,

Faye Drury

Faye Drury
Fourth-Grade Teacher

The opening in Model 3-4 explains the reason for the inquiry and tells the reader the writer has several questions. Some writers prefer to begin the letter with a direct question, such as "Can you give me the student test results for your district?" Other writers believe a question in the first sentence of an inquiry letter sounds overly abrupt, especially when writing to a stranger.

Body

- If you have several questions, number them so the reader can refer to them easily.
- With each question, add some explanatory detail to help the reader understand why you are asking this specific question.
- Avoid vague sentences that merely imply that you need some information, such as "I need to know about...."
- Avoid questions that can be answered with a simple *yes* or *no* unless that is the answer you actually want. "Do the chalkboards come in different sizes?" is not as useful as asking, "What sizes are available?"

The writer in Model 3-4 has numbered her questions and provided specific information about the student group with each question to help the reader respond appropriately.

Closing

- State a specific deadline for the response if you need the information for decision making.
- Express appreciation for the reader's help in answering your questions.
- Provide a telephone number, fax number, or e-mail address if those communication technologies are appropriate in your situation.

Invitations to Community Members

An invitation letter is a goodwill message asking the reader to attend a specific event or participate in some project. The letter can be addressed to an individual or to a group.

Purpose

As a goodwill message, the invitation letter suggests that the reader is someone whose presence or participation will be a valuable addition. The invitation also functions as a public relations message by informing

MODEL 3–4   Inquiry Letter

MONMOUTH HIGH SCHOOL
1200 Elm Drive
Memphis, Tennessee 38122
(901) 555-2243

October 17, 1999

Mr. Chad Ashenbach
Executive Director
Society of Media Associates
1636 Clay Parkway
Memphis, TN 38125

Dear Mr. Ashenbach:

We are planning our Senior Media Career Day programs for the spring semesters in 2001 and 2002, and we would like some information about the public relations media seminars your organization offers to groups. I have the following questions:

1. What is the preferred size of the group for a public relations media seminar? Our senior media group usually consists of 40 to 50 students, plus three advisors.

2. Can you tailor the seminar to begin at 9:00 a.m., include a lunch break of 1 hour and 15 minutes, and end at 3:00 p.m.? Part of the Career Day program includes a lunch at a nearby restaurant, and we try to simulate a business lunch environment.

3. Is a discount available for a school group? Career Day programs are funded through donations from local businesses, and we need to stretch our funds as far as possible.

We would appreciate answers to these questions in time for our planning meeting on November 15. If you have brochures available on the public relations media seminars, please enclose them with your response.

Sincerely,

Louisa Brooke

Louisa Brooke
English Department
Speech and Journalism

readers about important events connected to the school and its mission. In some cases, invitations are sent as a courtesy to influential people who can have an impact on school activities and funding. The writer may have little expectation that the receiver will accept the invitation, but the message reminds the reader of the school and its activities. Model 3-5 shows such an invitation. In most cases, however, the invitation goes to people who have a direct interest in the school's students and activities. Model 3-6 shows a typical invitation to parents.

MODEL 3–5   Invitation

TRAVIS ELEMENTARY SCHOOL
200 North Spring Drive
Amarillo, Texas 79111

October 2, 1999

The Honorable John C. Slocum
United States Senate
Washington, D.C. 20510

Dear Senator Slocum:

The students, faculty, and administrative staff of Travis Elementary School cordially invite you to our Fine Arts Pageant, April 19, 2000, at 2:00 p.m. in Dukes Auditorium. This annual event features poetry, plays, and music, all written and performed by our students. Student artwork will be displayed in the school lobby and hallways.

Our pageant has been a tradition for ten years and is attended by parents, business leaders, and community members. Students look forward to demonstrating their talents to interested guests.

We hope you will be able to join us on April 19, 2000, for another wonderful fine arts experience.

Very truly yours,

Stephanie J. Broadbent

Stephanie J. Broadbent
Principal

SJB/pd

MODEL 3–6   Invitation

NORTH COVE HIGH SCHOOL
890 County Line Road North Cove, Maine 04698
(207) 555-2748   Fax (207) 555-8759

October 10, 1999

Dear Parent or Guardian:

You are invited to celebrate **American Education Week** (November 1–5) with students, faculty, and administrative staff at a special breakfast program on November 3, 8:00 a.m. to 11:00 a.m. This year's theme is "The Future in Educational Technology."

The program will begin with a buffet breakfast in the school cafeteria at 8:00 a.m. Superintendent Jeffrey S. Corinthos will welcome visitors and speak briefly on district planning for educational technology. At 9:15 a.m. in the Auditorium, a panel of business leaders will discuss technology in their fields. The panel features Dr. Maria E. Lopez, Director of the Almont Wellness Center; Michael C. Russman, President, Tri-Tech Electronics, Inc.; and Georgia V. Swan, Project Manager, Northern Construction.

After the formal program, you will have an opportunity to meet with your child's teachers and counselors. We look forward to having you join us on November 3 at 8:00 a.m. for our celebration of **American Education Week.**

Sincerely,

Timothy L. Wilcock

Timothy L. Wilcock
Principal
TLW/rs

Organization

Write an invitation in the direct organization pattern and include specific information about events, times, dates, and other details that someone accepting the invitation will need to know. Follow these guidelines:

Opening

- State the invitation.
- Identify the event, date, time, and location in the opening paragraph.

Body

- Describe the event, naming activities, speakers, schedules, and the significance of the event.
- Select descriptive details that will interest your particular readers.

Closing

- Repeat your hope that the reader will accept the invitation.
- Repeat the time and date of a specific event.

Model 3-5 is a courtesy invitation to a senator, but the writer also mentions that parents and business and community leaders will be attending the pageant—information that might interest the senator. Model 3-6 offers parents a chance to meet with teachers and counselors in addition to the program activities—a further inducement to attending.

Permission Form Letters

Permission form letters are messages that inform parents about a planned activity that extends beyond the daily classroom, and the letters request formal parental permission for the child to participate. Parents must sign and return an attached form or a tear-off portion of the letter itself to indicate they have given permission.

Purpose

The permission letter is a legal document and a record for the school of the parent's decision about the child's participation in a field trip or other activity. A principal or other administrator usually writes the permission letter, which also informs parents about the purpose of the field trip and reasons for its inclusion in the curriculum. If the activity is more complicated than a simple field trip during a regular school day, parents should receive a separate itinerary or a detailed description of the event.

Permission letters must be clear and concise and provide enough information about the activity for parents to make informed decisions about allowing their children to participate.

Organization

Permission letters should always be on school letterhead. Use the direct organization pattern. Follow these guidelines:

Opening

- Use a subject line indicating the letter seeks permission for an activity or state this in the opening paragraph.
- State the exact nature of the outside classroom activity.
- State the date and purpose of the activity.

Body

- Explain the value or educational purpose of the activity.
- Assure the parents that the activity is safe and has adequate supervision.
- Avoid educational jargon in describing the activity.
- Maintain a positive tone.

Closing

- Remind the parents that they have the final authority to decide whether their child will participate.
- Tell the parents to sign and return the tear-off portion of the letter or the supplemental form.
- Specify the deadline for signing and returning the permission form.
- Explain what the child will do if parents do not give permission.
- Include the child's name, teacher's name, specific activity, date, and space for a parent's signature on the tear-off portion.

Model 3-7 is a typical permission letter. The writer uses a subject line to draw the reader's attention to the purpose of the letter. The opening paragraph identifies the field trip and states the school's commitment to field trips that enrich the curriculum. The middle paragraph adds further information about the usefulness of the trip and assures parents that adequate supervision will be in place. The closing sets a deadline for signing and returning the tear-off portion.

Model 3-8 is a variation of a permission letter. This letter asks parents to support the teacher in enforcing conduct rules. If parents sign the letter, they are agreeing to remind their children to obey the classroom conduct code. Telling the parents that the rules have been successful in the first half of the semester increases the likelihood that they will sign the pledge to support the rules.

Recommendation Letters

A recommendation letter supports someone's application for a new position or for special funding by favorably evaluating the person's potential

MODEL 3–7   Permission Form Letter

EISENHOWER ELEMENTARY SCHOOL
1400 Tammarck Road
Short Hills, NY 14855
(315) 555–2433

February 3, 1999

Dear Parent/Guardian:

Subject: **FIELD TRIP PERMISSION**

A field trip to the Short Hills Arboretum has been scheduled for
Tuesday, February 15, for the 5th grade. Eisenhower Elementary
School includes field trips in the curriculum because these
"classrooms without walls" enrich a child's learning.

The Short Hills Arboretum features an extensive collection of plants.
A visit there allows teachers to show students specimens covered in
their science units. All field trips are approved by the administration
and include five adults, in addition to participating teachers.

Please fill out and sign the form below to indicate permission for your
child's attendance and send it back to school with your child by
Wednesday, February 10. You are the final authority regarding
permission for your child to participate. Students who do not
participate in scheduled field trips complete library work units
related to the subject matter.

Sincerely,

Consuelo Pena

Consuelo Pena
Assistant Principal-Student Services

Student Name: _____

Nature of Field Trip: **Lecture/tour of Short Hills Arboretum**
Date of Field Trip: **February 15, 1999**
Teacher: _____
Yes, my child may participate _____
No, my child may not participate _____

Signature: _____

MODEL 3–8   Parental Support Form Letter

Mission Trail Elementary School
    504 Deerpath Road
        Lake Bluff, IL 60042
        (805) 555–0599

                  January 5, 1999

Dear Parents/Guardians:

Students benefit from reminders about behavior and rules when they return from holiday breaks to begin a new term. I would appreciate your help in maintaining a smooth transition from free time to structured class work.

Please review the attached CODE OF CONDUCT FOR ROOM 108 with your child. The class wrote these rules together in September; as a result, only two discipline reports were necessary between September and December.

If you have a convenient place to display the CODE at home, I would appreciate your doing so. I have a larger version displayed in the classroom, but your posting this CODE reinforces its importance. Also, your signing this letter and sending it back to school with your child will emphasize how we all support the behavior rules.

Thank you for your help. I welcome any questions or comments about your child's progress or our learning units in the months ahead.

                  Sincerely,

                  Jeannie Allenton
                  Jeannie Allenton
                  Grade 5, Room 108

I have read and reviewed the CODE OF CONDUCT RULES FOR ROOM 108 with my child.

Signature: _____

or past performance. A letter that supports giving an award to someone or that suggests someone for a position without the knowledge of the person involved is called a *nomination letter.* Both letters have the same purpose and organization.

Purpose

The recommendation letter provides hiring committees, scholarship committees, and potential employers with an outside evaluation of a person's scholastic and professional abilities and past performance in similar situations. Generally, people seek recommendation letters from those supervisors, teachers, or peers who will give favorable reports. Recommendation letters for top-level positions, such as superintendent, should be more than one page long.

Because of possible lawsuits over hiring decisions and the potential legal ramifications of any unfavorable personnel information, most people decline to write a recommendation letter if they cannot write a favorable one. Job applicants have a legal right to examine hiring materials, so recommendation letters are open to inspection. Rather than reveal any negative information, past employers usually write a brief statement indicating that the person was employed on specific dates for a specific position without including any evaluation of the work performance.

Employers and others seeking information may have to read between the lines. Notice the word choice in Model 3-9, a recommendation for a teacher. The writer uses the words "satisfactory" and "good" to describe the applicant's teaching, indicating mild but not enthusiastic support. The careful description of the applicant during faculty workshops as "active, even dominant" and "commenting forcefully" may hint at an aggressive personality. The closing suggestion that the writer will answer questions on the telephone implies that he has more to say but will do so only off the record.

In contrast, the closing paragraphs in Models 3-10, 3-11, and 3-12 are enthusiastic and stress the writer's regret at losing the person or the writer's confidence in the future success of the person.

Organization

Whether the recommendation letter is for a teacher, superintendent, student, or noncertified staff member, use the direct organization pattern. Follow these overall guidelines:

Opening

- Identify the person you are recommending and the position or award involved.
- Indicate your willingness to recommend the person.
- Summarize your overall recommendation of the person.
- State how long you have known the person and under what circumstances.

MODEL 3–9   Recommendation Letter for a Teacher

LICK CREEK COMMUNITY HIGH SCHOOL
405 School Road
Lick Creek, Indiana 47405
(317) 555–0900
March 31, 1999

Mr. Lawrence C. Hartwell
Superintendent
Bratten Consolidated School District
Highway 36 at Manheim Road
Bratten, IN 46567

Dear Mr. Hartwell:

As you may know, Craig Meyers has applied for the advertised full-time social studies position in your district. He has taught a two-thirds social studies schedule here for the past year, and he asked me to send you a letter of recommendation. I am happy to do so because he is a very dependable teacher.

Craig's teaching has been quite satisfactory. I observed his tenth grade class on two occasions, and he had good rapport with the students. His lesson plans are detailed with clear goals and age-appropriate classroom activities. In fact, two other social studies teachers have used some of his ideas in their own lesson plans. Craig's class record book is up to date, reflecting numerous student grades.

Craig has definite ideas about teaching. He was active, even dominant, in a series of faculty workshops devoted to disciplinary practice and classroom management strategies, and he commented forcefully on his ideas about a controlled classroom environment. He sets high standards for his students.

Craig was filling in here for two teachers who are returning in fall 1999, and we have no openings in the social studies area. I would be happy to answer any further questions if you would like to call me about Craig's application.

Sincerely,

Wynton S. Reismuth

Wynton S. Reismuth
Principal
WSR/cb

MODEL 3–10   Recommendation Letter for an Administrator

SCHOOL DISTRICT 131
BOARD OF EDUCATION
222 SPRING DRIVE
RIVERDALE, NY 10184
(607) 555–0987

January 23, 1999

Superintendent Search Committee and
Consultant to Board Members, School District 200
5566 Vista Valley Road
Dover Hills, NY 12944

I am happy to recommend Dr. Gregory Taggert for the position of
School District 200 Superintendent. I first met Dr. Taggert in 1993
at the American Association of School Administrators convention,
where we were on a panel together discussing school management
and urban disciplinary concerns. I was impressed at once with his
practical approach to school problems and his conviction that
problems represented opportunities to improve our schools. A year
later, I was delighted when he accepted the position of principal of
Hampton Valley High School.

As principal, Dr. Taggert has created a positive atmosphere for both
faculty and students during a difficult time of reorganization. His
favorite phrase, "Student learning and student services first," has
become the slogan of the student newspaper. He is efficient,
productive, and able to analyze situations and resolve problems
quickly.

Respected, soft-spoken, and very personable, Dr. Taggert relates well
to all members of the school community. Our district board members
have commented favorably many times on his handling of school
issues. His service during our annual hiring process has helped us
select appropriate teachers for our district, and I rely on his advice
for such hiring. I believe Dr. Taggert understands the political nature
of a superintendency, and we have talked frequently about national
educational trends.

He is active professionally, speaking regularly at regional and
national meetings. He serves on two state educational committees,
one on local funding issues and the other on finance management for
public schools. His undergraduate degree in accounting has helped
him understand and deal with school operations and financial issues

MODEL 3–10 *Continued*

Search Committee　　　　　　-2-　　　　　January 23, 1999
School District 200

as principal and probably has contributed to his interest in this
aspect of administration. Last year, he presented a paper on fiscal
management strategies for small schools with limited budgets. The
paper was revised as an article for <u>School Business</u> magazine,
scheduled to appear in the summer 1999 issue.

He is an effective planner and extremely organized in breaking down
large issues into smaller, more manageable tasks he can handle
effectively. Parents have commented favorably about school
efficiency since he became principal at Hampton Valley.

I would deeply regret losing Dr. Taggert, but I believe he is ready for
a superintendency. He is a superb communicator and administrator,
handling the demands of his building with great success and
maintaining rapport with faculty, staff, and students. He also is
experienced, dedicated, enthusiastic, and a consummate
professional. He has my highest recommendation; any school district
would be fortunate to have him as superintendent.

　　　　　　　　　　　　Sincerely,

　　　　　　　　　　　　Mathew L. Frenton

　　　　　　　　　　　　Mathew L. Frenton
　　　　　　　　　　　　Superintendent
　　　　　　　　　　　　Riverdale District 131

MLF/sh

Body

- Follow up positive comments, such as "He is excellent in the class-room," with a specific example.
- Respond directly to any specific questions asked about the person in an inquiry.
- Comment specifically about the person's abilities and interests that are relevant to the job or award.
- Explain any personal interaction, such as working on a project together or observing a teacher's class.
- Comment about relevant personality traits.

MODEL 3–11   Recommendation Letter for a Student

WILDWOOD HEIGHTS HIGH SCHOOL
3600 W. VALLEY DRIVE
WILDWOOD HEIGHTS, ILLINOIS 60047
(708) 555–3600

December 12, 1999

Dr. Clarissa Longridge
Chair, Freshman Challenge Scholarship Committee
Midwest Central University
University City, IA 50052

Dear Dr. Longridge:

I am writing in support of Amber Mitchell's application for a Freshman Challenge Scholarship for the 2000–2001 academic year. I have known Amber for four years, and I believe she is exactly the kind of student for whom the Freshman Challenge Scholarship was created.

Amber has been an outstanding student at Wildwood Heights High School. Her overall grade average in the accelerated program has never been lower than 3.85 on a 4-point scale. As advisor of our Big Sisters Club, I have worked closely with Amber for the two years she has been president. She has great energy and her creative ideas for reaching out to the middle school students have been well received by students and administrators.

I believe Amber would have been active in other groups as well if not for her home responsibilities. Her father died five years ago, and because her mother works full time to support the family, Amber has had a large role in caring for her two younger brothers and handling household duties. She has handled this heavy responsibility with cheerful determination. Her high grades indicate how much she values her education.

Amber Mitchell represents the very best of our young people today. She is bright, caring, and resourceful. She will be an asset to any university she attends.

Sincerely,

Suzanne Spencer

Suzanne Spencer
Social Studies Chairperson

MODEL 3–12   Recommendation Letter for Noncertified Staff

RICHLAND ELEMENTARY SCHOOL
6700 Springside Drive
Racine, Wisconsin 53106
(414) 555–9979

March 8, 1999

To Whom It May Concern:

Mary Jo Hansen-Roth has my enthusiastic recommendation for any position that requires her very special skills. As Administrative Assistant here since 1995, Ms. Hansen-Roth has displayed outstanding capabilities in organization, management, and communication.

Her position here required her to supervise two word processing specialists and three part-time clerical workers. She was extremely capable at organizing work and delegating tasks in ways that guaranteed completion of the regular work and any special projects. We allow subordinates to rate their supervisors on an annual basis, and Ms. Hansen-Roth's ratings were always in the range of 4.6 on a 5-point scale. Her communication skills are excellent. She wrote and produced our monthly newsletter and wrote nearly all the form letters that went out under my name.

I believe Ms. Hansen-Roth will be an asset to any firm that employs her. We are all sorry she has decided to leave this area and move to the Southwest, but we wish her the greatest success.

Sincerely,

Trisha L. Pendergast

Trisha L. Pendergast
Principal

TLP/lt

Closing

- Repeat your overall recommendation.
- Indicate that you are unhappy to lose the person or that you would be glad to rehire the person if true.
- Use your full title in your signature block.

Consider which features are most important for a position, and discuss those in your recommendation. The mild recommendation for the teacher in Model 3-9 mentions his superior lesson plans. Model 3-11 refers to the student overcoming difficult personal circumstances. Model 3-10 reviews the superintendent's abilities in several areas. Model 3-12 stresses the administrative assistant's capabilities in organization and communication.

Superintendent or top-level administrator recommendations should include the following:

- Communication skills
- Ability to deal with diverse communities
- Experience in interviewing and hiring
- Professional participation in conferences or publication
- Expertise in school–community relations
- Experience in dealing with school finances and funding issues
- Educational philosophy
- Administrative and supervisory style
- Personality

Teacher recommendations should mention the following:

- Classroom management style
- Instructional style
- Organization and planning (grade book, lesson plans)
- Classroom discipline style
- Use of curriculum guidelines, grade-level goals and objectives
- Personal observations of classes
- Professional involvement, such as attending conferences or special teaching workshops
- Communication style
- Work on collaborative projects
- Response by students and parents

Student recommendations should mention the following:

- Academic achievements
- Extracurricular activities
- Potential for success
- Leadership capabilities
- Personal circumstances that the student has overcome

- Personality
- The writer's personal involvement with the student as a teacher, counselor, or supervisor

Noncertified staff recommendations should mention the following:

- Ability to work on a team
- Ability to meet deadlines
- Efficiency in organizing work
- Supervisory style
- Personality
- Official evaluation reports
- Communication skills
- Interaction with students, parents, or community members
- Personal interaction with the staff member as a supervisor or when working on a project

Another person's future may depend on the recommendation letter you write; consider carefully how to present the person's best qualities in a positive evaluation.

Requests to Community Members

Requests are persuasive appeals for some tangible contribution, such as time or money, to the school's programs or physical plant.

Purpose

The purpose of the request letter is to persuade the reader to cooperate and agree to do what the writer asks. The writer must supply enough information to allow the reader to make a decision and must anticipate any objections in order to counter them while explaining the request. A persuasive request should also build a favorable image for the school by noting past successes and ways in which the new request will build on that success.

The request uses two basic appeals: *factual* and *emotional*. The factual appeal explains the situation, includes appropriate statistics and background, and provides specific information about needed equipment, systems, or programs. The emotional appeal stresses how good the reader will feel after helping the school or the importance of individual effort in educational programs for the younger members of the community. These two appeals often work together. A letter asking business leaders to contribute to a job training program can stress both the state-of-the-art training and also the overall satisfaction in helping students develop into good potential employees. Even if a business executive never hires any graduates of the program, his or her contribution has served the community as a whole.

A request letter should focus on the immediate need, such as getting the reader to attend a planning meeting. If a writer stresses a goal too distant or too abstract, the reader may think immediate action is unnecessary.

Organization

The organization of a request letter may involve a direct request in the opening paragraph or a delayed request, depending on how cooperative you think the reader will be. If you expect some resistance from the reader, delay the request until you have explained the circumstances and presented a case for contributions. Because you are writing to a person who is not expecting your letter, you must introduce the situation, explain its importance, and convince the reader to become involved. Consider these elements:

Opening

- Attract the reader's attention with interesting information related to the school and the project about which you are writing.
- State your request directly.

Both Models 3-13 and 3-14 are direct requests and state the request in the opening. However, Model 3-15 thanks the readers for their past contributions and delays the new request until the end of the third paragraph.

Body

- Explain the project or reason for the request in detail.
- Explain how the reader can contribute to this project.
- Stress the benefits to the students and community.
- State any required meeting times, dates, or length of volunteer service, as when asking someone to chaperone a dance.
- Explain that money spent now will save money in the future.
- Explain that time spent now will enhance the students' education in the future.
- Show that costs are reasonable based on the benefits.

MODEL 3–13   **Letter Requesting Service**

ROBERT E. LEE HIGH SCHOOL
800 S. Shady Tree Boulevard
Ravenwood, South Carolina 37055

(803) 555–9191
Fax (803) 555–9291

August 12, 1999

Mr. Jefferson S. Trent
President
Mercury Sporting Equipment
700 Western Road
Ravenwood, SC 37054

Dear Mr. Trent:

The education of Ravenwood's children has been strengthened because of the support you and other business leaders have given to the activities and goals of our educational programs. We need the expertise of business leaders for updating school policies. Would you be willing to serve on the Robert E. Lee High School Policy Committee for the school year 1999–2000?

The Policy Committee meets on the first Wednesday evening of every month at 7:00 p.m. in the school lounge. The first meeting of this school year will be Wednesday, September 6. The committee usually is composed of a Ravenwood business leader, the department chairs, volunteer parents/guardians, and students. I chair the committee. Generally, we consider all aspects of curriculum revisions, testing programs, codes of conduct, disciplinary trends, school safety, and any new issues that develop or that are mandated by the school superintendent.

Your contributions to our policy planning would be invaluable. Please consider accepting a seat on this committee. You will be doing a great service to the 1,200 students here and the future of education in Ravenwood.

Sincerely,

Victoria P. Ashley

Victoria P. Ashley
Principal

VPA/cg

MODEL 3–14 Letter Requesting a Contribution

MANDAN HILLS HIGH SCHOOL
180 Snake River Road
Mandan Hills, Idaho 83211
(208) 555–1600

April, 13 1999

Mr. Timothy P. Bratten
President
Mountain Gorge Construction Co.
1300 Snake River Road
Mandan Hills, ID 83211

Dear Mr. Bratten:

As you probably know, our Mandan Hills Comets won the 1998
Region II Soccer Championship—the first championship in soccer for
our school. We have great confidence in our chances to repeat the
championship next season and would like you to be a part of our
success by contributing to the Mandan Hills Booster Club, targeting
your donation for soccer.

If you support our soccer teams and want to help defray the costs of
camps and workshops, please consider sending a donation to the
"Mandan Hills High School Soccer Comets." In this way, you will help
provide our soccer teams with options to improve their skills and
techniques, options not otherwise available.

In addition, you will contribute to the overall community support for
Mandan Hills teams, which we believe was instrumental in our team
members attending several excellent soccer camps. Please return the
enclosed card or call me at 555–1600 if you have any questions.

Sincerely,

Jeffery Greyeagle

Jeffery Greyeagle
Soccer Coach

Because Model 3-15 is an indirect request, the second paragraph
continues the appreciation of the first paragraph and stresses the benefits gained from the reader's previous contribution. The third paragraph
presents the new project, explaining why the school needs it. After that

MODEL 3–15   Letter Requesting a Contribution

BLACK HILLS ACADEMY
200 Elk Road
Sioux River, South Dakota 57003
(605) 555–2324

September 1, 1999

Mr. and Mrs. Gordon Haskell
1600 Hickory Lane
Sioux River, SD 57003

Dear Mr. and Mrs. Gordon Haskell:

Thank you for your contribution last year in our fund-raising to install computers in all our classrooms. Over the summer, we purchased and installed a bank of computers in every classroom, and students are now using them to access the Internet and enhance research projects and independent study.

Our sixth grade is gathering information from company web sites about marketing products internationally. The fourth graders are learning about banking procedures through Internet sites. These activities would not be possible without your help.

Black Hills Academy is now focusing efforts on improving the recreational opportunities for our younger students. The board has decided to install a soft surface playground and new play equipment on the south lawn. Since the Academy instituted a kindergarten program two years ago, we have discovered that the littler students need a special area for recess and physical activity programs. We are asking for your help again in contributing to a special fund for a soft surface playground and equipment.

Complete details about the proposed playground and equipment will be sent to you shortly. Please consider the information and how you can join this effort. We deeply appreciate the contributions of parents in making our school the finest in the region.

Sincerely,

Kyle T. Whitman

Kyle T. Whitman
Academic Dean

KTW/dd

explanation, the writer requests contributions. By withholding the request until after the explanation, the writer hopes the reader will understand the need for the project and agree to help.

Closing

- Ask specifically for the action you want.
- Mention any deadlines involved.
- Provide a means for further discussion, such as your telephone number.
- If appropriate, express appreciation for past contributions.
- Assure the reader of the importance of his or her contribution.

Model 3-13 stresses the benefit to the student body and future education in the community. Model 3-14 focuses on the soccer team and its expected success. Model 3-15 asks the readers to consider the project and promises more detailed information shortly. This closing emphasizes the readers' past contributions and gives them credit for the success of the school in general.

A persuasive request must develop common ground between the writer and the reader. Usually, this common ground is the belief in the importance of education and interest in the welfare and success of the students. (See also "Persuasive Messages" in Chapter 2 and "Requests of School Personnel" in Chapter 3.)

Responses to Complaints from Community Members

A response to a complaint is a message designed to overcome the receiver's negative experience or impression. Complaints cover a wide variety of topics. In one day, a principal may hear from a mother who says her child did not get a cheese squirt on his hamburger at lunchtime, a neighbor who complains that he saw two teachers hitting softballs before the end of the school day, and a community leader who objects to a school policy. All these complaints may require a response letter.

Purpose

The response to a complaint must explain the school circumstances in such a way as to erase the original negative impression and rebuild the reader's confidence in the school and its officials. Often, the writer can make an adjustment that will satisfy the complainant, such as telling the mother her child will get an extra cheese squirt during the next lunch period. In other cases, the writer must explain a situation so the reader understands and accepts it.

No matter how trivial the complaint, write your response with the idea of improving relations with the complainant. Your letter should be reasonable, calm, and positive, even if the complainant is highly agitated or abusive. Maintain a positive, thoughtful tone; stress any benefits resulting from a policy or activity; and leave the reader with the impression that you have carefully considered the complaint and are responding seriously.

Organization

Use the direct organization pattern for a response to a complaint. Follow these guidelines:

Opening

- State your concern for the reader's view of the situation.
- Mention the date of an incoming letter or telephone call about the situation.
- Never repeat the negative characterization of the situation used by the person who complained.
- Use neutral language, such as "the episode," rather than a negative term, such as "the food fight."
- Do not describe a negative incident in any detail.
- Mention any official circumstances, such as a school policy, local law, government regulation, or national school standard.

Body

The middle paragraphs should explain the factors involved in the situation.

- Explain the context of the situation, such as official decisions, new educational standards, new laws, or a circumstance causing the situation.
- Mention any higher official with authority responsible for decision making, or quote an official or a relevant law or policy.
- Explain why the circumstances are a benefit to students or the educational process.
- Do not sound defensive or dismissive.
- Show how policies or laws benefit and protect students.
- Explain why the circumstances are necessary at this time.
- Explain why the circumstances may change in the future.

- Describe any personal knowledge or experience in the matter.
- Identify other schools or districts that have similar situations.

Closing

- Assure the reader that the situation is under control or being handled appropriately.
- Use a positive tone both about the situation and about your confidence that the school and its programs are not negatively affected.
- Invite the reader to discuss the matter further if circumstances change or deteriorate.
- If appropriate, tell the reader when a specific change is expected.

Model 3-16 shows a response to a mother's complaint about the "prison atmosphere" at a high school with newly installed metal detector canopies and hand-held metal detectors. The writer identifies the subject and mentions the mother's "concern" but does not repeat her negative comments. The writer points out that the detectors are a result of a Board of Education policy, mentions the date, and quotes an excerpt from the policy. The middle paragraphs of Model 3-16 reassure the mother that the school has not had violent episodes and the detectors are a preventive measure. The writer mentions his own observation of the security system and identifies other school districts that are also adding detectors to school buildings. He also stresses the safety benefit. The closing paragraph repeats the district's commitment to safety, and the writer expresses confidence about the security measures. Overall, the writer's tone is serious, but reassuring, to the mother.

(See also "Maintaining Positive Tone" in Chapter 2.)

Responses to Inquiries from Community Members

A letter that responds to an inquiry may provide data the reader has asked for or explain a situation so the reader understands it.

Purpose

The primary purpose of the response to an inquiry is to satisfy the reader's interest in a particular subject. The letter also functions as a goodwill message because the writer can present the school in a favorable light while answering the reader's question. Do not overlook an opportunity to include positive information even if the reader did not directly ask for it. For example, while answering questions about the

MODEL 3–16   Response to a Complaint Letter

WEST CENTRAL HIGH SCHOOL
677 De Leon Avenue
Miami, Florida 33140
(305) 555–8767

September 6, 1999

Mrs. Romona Hicks
6211 E. Beach Street
Miami, FL 33140

Dear Mrs. Hicks:

I appreciate the concern you expressed in your letter of September 2 about our newly installed metal detector security canopies and the hand-held detectors our security monitors use when they greet buses and arriving students. These increased security measures are part of the District 80 Board of Education policy, passed August 10, 1999, "to guarantee the safety of all students in our school buildings."

The Board's policy was based on a determination to prevent any violent episodes such as those that have occurred elsewhere nationwide. No West Central students have been discovered carrying weapons or have been involved in violence on school property. We believe the metal detectors act as a deterrent to any students tempted to act inappropriately or dangerously. The metal detector canopies monitor anyone who walks beneath them. I have personally observed students arriving every morning since the term began on August 28, and I assure you that the security check does not delay the students' entry into the building or interfere with normal activities.

Currently, two adjoining districts, Seacliff and Edgewater, are also installing metal detectors as a preventive measure. The detectors are especially valuable in alerting school officials if nonstudents attempt to enter the building while carrying weapons.

The Board of Education and West Central's administrators and faculty are committed to providing a safe environment where your child and others can concentrate on learning.

Sincerely,

Wilton P. Epson

Wilton P. Epson
Principal

WPE/rh

planned renovations to the gymnasium, a writer might include information about the winning basketball team.

Organization
Use the direct organization pattern. If you are unable to answer the reader's inquiry, you should explain why (such as enrollment reports are not available) and state when you will be able to provide the information. If the information is confidential, tell the reader that and explain why confidentiality is important in this instance. If you can answer the inquiry, follow these guidelines:

Opening
- Answer a simple inquiry at once, or state that you are happy to answer the reader's questions.
- Identify the date of the inquiry within a statement about the topic. Avoid a full sentence that merely states you received an inquiry. The first sentence in Model 3-17 identifies the reader's letter while also identifying the topic and expressing pleasure at the inquiry.

Body
- If the reader asked a series of questions, answer them in the same order as asked.
- If the inquiry involved numbered questions or specific topical headings, number your answers to match or use the same topical headings as your reader did.
- If any negative information is involved, avoid using negative terms and condense the information to avoid emphasis. Do not begin or end a paragraph with negative information.

Closing
- Include extra positive information in your answer.
- Maintain a friendly tone, implying that you are happy to respond and are glad the reader is interested in your school.

Model 3-17 is a letter responding to an inquiry about a student volunteer at a nursing home. The writer takes the opportunity to explain the service-learning program in detail and to stress the expected benefits to the community. This response becomes a goodwill message that the reader may share with others. (See also "Good News or Information Messages" in Chapter 2.)

MODEL 3–17   Response to an Inquiry Letter

LINCOLN HIGH SCHOOL
650 Lincoln Parkway
Center City, Kansas 66555
(316) 555-1212

October 4, 1999

Mrs. Amelia Lockett
168 S. Mission Drive
Center City, KS 66555

Dear Mrs. Lockett:

I was delighted to receive your letter of October 1, praising one of
our students for her work at the Golden Sunset Nursing Facility, and
I am glad to answer your questions about our new service-learning
project.

On September 15, 1999, Lincoln High School students began
performing special community service to fulfill the new Student
Community Service requirement passed by the Center City Board of
Education in April 1999. Starting this school year, all Lincoln High
School students must complete 20 hours of community service
during their junior or senior year in order to graduate. Students have
a variety of service options:

- Visiting nursing homes, helping direct the residents in art or
  discussion activities, leading in sing-alongs
- Clearing and maintaining pathways in Governor's Park
- Preparing or serving holiday meals at Midtown Mission
- Collecting, sorting, wrapping, and distributing holiday toys to
  needy children or collecting, boxing, and delivering holiday
  food boxes to needy families

Advisors monitor student activities at the approved sites, and
guidelines ensure student safety.

The student who helped your mother with her correspondence was
one of these seniors fulfilling her community service. We expect your
mother's pleasant experience will be only one of the many significant
benefits of this program.

Sincerely,

Mitchell Kestner

Mitchell Kestner
Principal

MK/jp

Responses to Requests from Community Members

A letter responding to a reader's specific request provides an answer and explanation of the answer to the reader.

Purpose

The response to a request may be good news (you agree to the request) or bad news (you refuse the request) for the reader. In either case, the letter should strive for as much goodwill as possible by maintaining a pleasant, reasonable tone. Include appropriate positive information about the school, faculty, students, and programs.

Organization

If you are granting the request, use the direct organization pattern because the reader will be happy to receive the news in the opening paragraph. If you are refusing the request, use the indirect organization pattern because you want the reader to understand your reasons and the situation before receiving the refusal. Follow these guidelines:

Granting the Request

Opening

- Grant the request immediately.
- Identify relevant dates, times, and places. The opening sentence in Model 3-18 grants the request and confirms the date of the request, the date of the conference, and the full name of the organization.

Body

- Explain any relevant background, conditions, or arrangements connected to the request. The writer in Model 3-18 confirms the date of the request, the date of the conference, and full name of the organization.
- Explain any relevant benefits. Model 3-18 explains the potential benefit to students and emphasizes this benefit as the reason for granting the request.

Closing

- Remind the reader of relevant deadlines and necessary arrangements.
- Explain any action the reader must perform.
- Include a telephone number, fax number, or e-mail as a courtesy.

MODEL 3–18   Positive Response to a Request Letter

HENRY CLAY MIDDLE SCHOOL
170 Jackson Parkway
Lexington, Kentucky 40507
(606) 555–6586

February 6, 1999

Ms. Jennifer E. Heath
7800 Perryville Lane
Lexington, KY 40507

Dear Ms. Heath:

Henry Clay Middle School will be happy to host the opening general session of the Kentucky Writers' Conference, May 16, as you requested in your letter of January 28.

When I received your letter, I consulted the faculty and our local writers who will judge our spring writing contest, and all agreed that hearing writers talk about their craft would be an appropriate activity for our sixth, seventh, and eighth-grade Language Arts classes. The chance to see and hear some of Kentucky's serious writers will be an enriching experience and should encourage our students to work on their own writing.

Our auditorium seats 500. You indicated that you expect about 200 people to attend the conference, so there will be room for students to attend as well. I am reserving the auditorium for May 16 for your group. Please contact me at 555–6586 to make further arrangements. I look forward to meeting you.

Sincerely,

Mary F. Arnold

Mary F. Arnold
Principal

MFA:st

The closing in Model 3-18 reminds the reader that further discussion is needed and confirms the reservation of the auditorium for the group.

Refusing the Request

Opening

- Establish a pleasant and concerned tone in the opening paragraph, but do not reveal your decision. In Model 3-19 the writer agrees in principle with the reader but does not reveal his decision.

Body

- Explain the reasons for the situation, the conditions affecting the situation, any governmental regulations, and any background for previous decisions about the topic. Model 3-19 explains how home-room assignments are made.
- Connect the refusal to the reasons you have explained.

Closing

- Offer an alternative if available, a possible change in the future if appropriate, or a goodwill comment. Model 3-19 offers to reconsider the request at a later date.

Careful word choice is necessary when refusing requests. Do not use any words implying that the reader is making an unreasonable request or is unable to understand the situation. Notice the careful word choice in the closing sentence of Model 3-19. The writer's use of "possible arrangements" and "whenever we can" indicate that the refusal may stand. (See also "Good News or Information Messages" and "Bad News Messages" in Chapter 2 and "Responses to Requests from School Personnel" in Chapter 3.)

Thank-You Letters

Thank-you letters are goodwill messages of appreciation sent to those people who voluntarily helped the writer, the students, or the school in some way.

Purpose

The thank-you letter is an important message and courtesy to people who have volunteered their time, money, or energies to enhancing the educational institution or experience. Write a thank-you letter within three days of the conclusion of the person's volunteer work. Informally

MODEL 3–19 **Negative Response to a Request Letter**

GREAT LAKES HIGH SCHOOL
6700 S. Michigan Avenue
Chicago, IL 60630

(312) 555–1199
Fax (312) 555–1919

November 18, 1999

Mrs. Francine Harris
7800 S. Michigan Avenue
Chicago, IL 60030

Dear Mrs. Harris:

I certainly agree with you that a student's learning environment is one of the most important elements in the educational process.

When I received your note on October 16, I immediately checked homeroom assignments and the numbers of students in each homeroom. We make homeroom assignments at the beginning of the school year based on enrollment and alphabetical listing of students' names. Talesha was assigned Room 162 with Mr. Jones as part of the overall distribution of students. Moving one student requires moving a series of students, which would disrupt student schedules this far into the semester. Therefore, Talesha's homeroom assignment will have to remain as it is for the rest of the semester.

Some student transfers occur during the holiday break before the second semester, and some homeroom assignments may be changed. I am placing your letter in my follow-up file, so I can reconsider Talesha's homeroom assignment then. We are always interested in making the best possible arrangements for our students whenever we can.

Sincerely,

Ronald P. Winters

Ronald P. Winters
Assistant Principal

RPW/et

expressing appreciation to the person at the time of the event or favor is not a substitute for a written thank-you letter.

Organization
Use the direct organization pattern for thank-you letters. Keep the letter brief and focused on the relevant actions for which you are thanking the reader. Follow these guidelines:

Opening
- Thank the reader.
- Identify the nature of the favor or contribution.
- Mention the specific date of the reader's contribution.

Body
- Mention some positive result from the person's efforts.

Closing
- Repeat your thanks.

Model 3-20 is a typical thank-you letter. The writer indicates that the laboratory tour had lasting positive effects.

MEMOS

Memos represent formal communication with members of your school district. The tone and attitude expressed in memos should create a mutually cooperative atmosphere because readers and writers share the same overall goals for the schools and district.

Announcements to School Personnel

Announcements provide information about events, activities, and administrative decisions to faculty and staff or other members of the school district.

Purpose
Although the grapevine in any school is usually very active, an official announcement ensures that all parties involved in or affected by a situation receive the same information about events, such as details about

MODEL 3–20   Thank-You Letter

ST. JOHN'S ELEMENTARY SCHOOL
78 Chambers Drive
Mount Henry, NY 11791
(518) 555–2929

May 10, 1999

Ms. Laurie T. Schneider
Public Relations Director
Reese Laboratory
1400 S. Woodwind Avenue
Mount Henry, NY 11792

Dear Ms. Schneider:

Thank you so much for arranging and leading a tour through the blood testing unit of Reese Laboratory on May 9. My sixth-grade class thoroughly enjoyed the visit.

The students were especially excited about having their blood typed, and several parents have called to indicate that they think the visit was a valuable one.

My students and I appreciate your taking the time to enhance our science studies. And I expect to take advantage of your kind offer to host another visit next year.

Sincerely,

Monica P. Kimball

Monica P. Kimball
Sixth-Grade Teacher

---

date, time, place, and participants. Official announcements about administrative decisions provide the background and the rationale, and they may clarify who or what group is responsible for the decision. Faculty and staff also write announcements about upcoming events or activities. Clear memo announcements remind school personnel about changes or developments, discourage rumors, offset potential uncertainty about the future, and remind readers what is expected of them. Announcements also enhance administrator–faculty relationships by providing a predictable form of reliable communication that bolsters morale and good building climate.

Internal announcements to faculty, staff, and students are usually memos. Depending on the subject, the memos may be placed in appropriate school mailboxes, with a copy posted on the faculty lounge bulletin board and in department offices.

Do not combine announcements about different events in one memo. Readers are likely to overlook one of the events or confuse details about them. Individual announcements about each event or decision are easiest to read and understand.

Organization

Internal announcements usually are written in the direct organization pattern with the basic information in the opening paragraph. Model 3-21 announces a guest speaker in the first paragraph, along with date and time. Because the event is a positive one, the opening also conveys enthusiasm. Follow these guidelines:

Subject Line

- Refer to a specific subject.
- Avoid general subject lines, such as "News" or "Items to Consider." Busy faculty and staff may postpone reading such memos because the subject line does not indicate an issue they recognize as relevant.

Opening

- Identify the specific event or decision.
- Identify date, time, and place for an event.
- State the full name and title of a visitor.
- State the general purpose of an event or program.

Body

- Provide detailed information about the event. Model 3-21 identifies the teacher who arranged the centenarian's visit to the school. The writer also provides a paragraph of information that teachers can relate to their students to help prepare for this speaker's visit.

Closing

- Tell the readers what the next step will be or how the announcement will affect the future. The closing paragraph in Model 3-21 has an enthusiastic tone and urges teachers to prepare students for the special event.

MODEL 3–21   Announcement Memo

To: Faculty and Staff

From: Daryl Harris   *DH*
            Principal

Date: April 10, 1999

Re: Special Assembly, Guest Speaker Mrs. Maybelle Jones

I am delighted to announce that we will have a very special guest speaker on **Tuesday, April 24, at 9:30 a.m. in the gymnasium.** Mrs. Maybelle Jones, a resident of our community for 100 years, will speak to all members of our school about her experiences and answer questions about her life and times.

We owe this extraordinary event to the efforts of phys ed's Darlene Wilks. Darlene met Mrs. Jones at a church supper and realized immediately that she would be both fascinating to our students and an inspiration to them.

Please tell your students that Mrs. Jones was born here in Wilmington in 1899. Her grandfather was born a slave in Georgia in 1861, but the family moved here immediately after the Civil War. Mrs. Jones worked at Hammet Manufacturing for 37 years before retiring and still attends Heritage Baptist Church regularly. She has 49 grandchildren, great-grandchildren and great-great grandchildren. She visits her relatives frequently and enjoys reading and baking. I have talked to her and found her utterly delightful and an amazing woman, and I know our students will agree.

Classes will be dismissed by announcement, and teachers will lead students to assigned seating areas. Since Mrs. Jones is slightly deaf, we will use floor microphones to allow students to ask her questions. Jim Fenton will handle the microphones.

Let's get our students ready to appreciate this opportunity to hear our community's history from someone who experienced events we can only read about.

(See also "Good News or Information Messages" in Chapter 2 and "Announcements and Flyers" in Chapter 5.)

Confidential Memos

A confidential memo can cover any topic, but most frequently it deals with an emergency situation or a special student situation. The writer intends the memo only for those directly addressed in the heading. The memo is usually stamped at the top as "confidential," and it is sent in an envelope marked "confidential." If the writer does not use an envelope, the memo is folded, stapled shut, and marked "confidential" on the outside. If the writer wants to be certain that an administrator's secretary does not see the message, he or she should deliver it personally to the administrator or specifically tell the secretary that the message is for the administrator only. The writer may conclude the memo with the directive "Destroy After Reading."

Purpose

The purpose of a confidential memo may include the following:

- To explain a personal matter to an administrator
- To announce unscheduled or anticipated disaster drills
- To explain how an emergency or family crisis is affecting a student's work
- To announce additional security officers on duty or a police canine unit for a locker check during a specific time
- To explain the presence of an ambulance or police on school property
- To announce a "code red" security alert for a bomb threat or when someone has been seen with a weapon
- To announce organized, but unauthorized, student protests, demonstrations, or other disturbances
- To explain a personnel problem

Organization

Use the direct organization pattern for all subjects because you want the reader to understand the situation at once. In some cases, immediate action is required. Follow these guidelines:

Opening

- Identify the subject in the subject line.
- State the main information. Model 3-22 tells the readers that a student is having a family crisis.
- Identify relevant people or events.

MODEL 3–22   Confidential Memo about a Student

CONFIDENTIAL MEMO

To: John Arnold
           Melinda Carnes-Reeder
           Dolores Morales
           Janelle Patterson
           Joe Vasquez
           Keith Watkins

From: Margery Fletcher   *MF*
           Guidance Office

Subject: Tiffini Levinson—Father's Illness

As Tiffini Levinson's teachers, you should know that her father is
very ill. Mrs. Levinson, Tiffini's mother, has informed me that the
first-floor dining room has been converted to a hospital-style
bedroom with medical equipment and intravenous lines. Visiting
nurses come daily. Mrs. Levinson said her husband is not expected
to recover from his illness.

Please be patient with Tiffini during this difficult period. She is very
close to her father and spends several hours a day reading to him.
Alert me immediately if you see any extreme changes in her
behavior or academic work.

If you would like to discuss Tiffini's work with me, please stop by my
office. I will update you as I learn more.

Body

- Provide any necessary background or specific directions, such as steps to take for a sudden severe-weather warning.
- State specifically any actions you want the readers to take.
- If the memo concerns an investigation of an incident that could involve legal charges, do not reveal a student's identity.

Closing

- Offer to discuss the matter further. Model 3-22 offers discussion and promises updates as more information develops.

The confidential memo is usually short with clear, short sentences and short paragraphs. Reserve extended discussion of a subject for other correspondence or personal meetings.

Instructions to School Personnel

Instructions explain to readers how to perform a sequence of steps in a given action or how to handle certain materials or systems without any sequence of actions involved.

Purpose

Instructions are necessary in many instances to guide people through new activities. Three possible situations require instructions. First, one person must perform the steps of an action in sequence, such as filling out detention forms. Second, several people must perform an action together, such as supervising the Saturday college exams or conducting a demonstration for visitors at an Open House. Third, one or more persons must perform actions or follow guidelines, but not in any sequence, such as supervising the science fair or monitoring inside suspensions.

To write effective instructions, consider your readers and how much they know about the subject. In most cases, assume that your readers need precise guidance in performing actions or handling systems. Do not skip steps and assume readers will fill in missing information.

Readers need consistency in instructions. Follow these guidelines for language:

- Keep parallel structure in lists. Be sure that each item in a list is in the same grammatical form. The actions in Model 3-23 listed under "Faculty in Classrooms" all begin with verbs. In Model 3-24, the first list covers locations; the second list covers circumstances. Each list is parallel because the items fit the category and phrases are structured similarly.
- Use the same term for an item throughout the instructions. Do not refer to "rotating schedule" in one step and "shifting schedule" in another step when you mean the same thing.
- Use precise details. The *west side of the building* is more exact than the *left side of the building* or the *shaded side of the building*.

Organization

Begin instructions with an introduction explaining the purpose of the instructions and for whom they are intended. Many school instructions

MODEL 3–23   Instruction Sheet

INSTRUCTIONS FOR OPEN HOUSE ACTIVITIES

Faculty in Classrooms:

- Greet each visitor and ask the visitor to sign the guest book.
- Give each adult visitor a copy of the Open House brochure.
- Give each child one of the cardboard figures of Chief Osceola.
- Demonstrate the video equipment with the tape showing construction of our building.
- Allow students to demonstrate their computer skills.
- Invite visitors to comment in the "Visitor Remarks" book.

Building Tour Guides

Conduct tours in the following order:

1. Central lobby area
2. Auditorium
3. Central back stairway to second floor
4. Reading and language laboratory
5. Classroom 202
6. Central front stairway down to first floor

Outdoor Grounds Guides

Visitors will gather at the west side of the building.

Stan Levine	1.	Describe playground and new equipment.
	2.	Demonstrate the double-bolt security gates.
Lauren Bell	3.	Explain recess system.
	4.	Explain age-appropriate activities.
Stan Levine	5.	Invite visitors to try hitting balls into softball/ junior football field.
Lauren Bell	6.	Walk visitors around tennis court and mini track.

---

are given in memos. If the instructions are on a separate sheet, a cover memo can also provide an introduction. Instructions are organized in one of three ways:

> **Sequential steps**—Steps that should be performed in sequence should be numbered. Notice the section for "Building Tour Guides" in Model 3-23. The areas are listed in the order the guides are to visit them.

MODEL 3–24   Instruction Memo

To: Faculty and Staff

From: Kenneth Yamaguchi   *KY*
             Assistant Principal

Date: August 27, 1999

Re: Attendance Instruction

As we begin the new school year, I thought it best to review the instructions for marking attendance. As a general rule, the student must be present for at least half of the class period to be counted as present. Following are specific rules.

Do not mark a student absent if the student is called to any of the following:

- guidance office
- assistant principal's office
- principal's office
- dean's office

Mark a student as absent under the following conditions:

- student is sick in bathroom or in nurse's office
- student is in office for disciplinary action
- student went to an administrator's office on his/her own
- student was on vacation with parents
- student was making a nonpermitted phone call

Please note that an administrator may issue an official excuse for the student in any of the above circumstances.

Please follow these rules when filling out the attendance forms to ensure consistency in our attendance data. Thanks for your enthusiastic response to our in-service program last week. Let's have a great year at McKinley High!

Nonsequential guidelines—Steps that do not have to be performed in a particular order are highlighted with bullets or some other device. Numbering would imply sequence. Notice that the section for "Faculty in Classrooms" in Model 3-23 has actions highlighted by bullets. These actions do not have to be performed in order. The instructions in Model 3-24 cover several circumstances, only one of which will be relevant at a time. The writer uses bullets because chronology is not a factor in these instructions.

Sequential steps for people—When people work together to perform an action, use a "playscript" format with a person listed in a column on the left and the relevant action listed on the same line in a column on the right. Notice that Model 3-23, "Outdoor Grounds Guides," uses playscript format to show how two people will handle the outdoor tour. The steps are numbered sequentially from beginning to end no matter how many people are involved and no matter how many actions one individual performs. (See also "Policy Statements and Procedures" in Chapter 5.)

Requests of School Personnel

An internal request often asks for specific information, such as class counts, numbers of failing grades, absences, and other data. An internal request may also be an appeal for cooperation in some way that will support the school's goals and programs. The request may be from the administration to the faculty and staff or the reverse. Faculty and staff may also write requests of each other. When asking for information, explain why the information is needed. When asking for cooperation, use a persuasive tone and emphasize reader benefits. Administrators should avoid requests that sound dictatorial and harsh.

Purpose
The purpose of the internal request is to gather information or persuade the reader to act or make a decision. Assume that the readers share the school and district goals, and present the request in terms of how it supports those goals. Emphasize the reasons for the request and provide sufficient instructions so readers can comply easily.

Organization
Use the direct organization pattern for internal requests. Follow these guidelines:

Opening
- Identify the general situation.
- State your request directly as in Model 3-25.

MODEL 3–25   Request Memo

To: Faculty

From: Maria Cincinni   *MC*
           Coordinator, Reading and ESL

Date: September 4, 1999

Re: Speech and Language Screenings

Because we have had such a large freshman enrollment this fall, I
need your help in beginning the necessary speech and language
screenings. These screenings are the basis for directing students into
special programs to improve their speech and language skills.

Please take a few minutes to prescreen all your freshmen by
listening to their speech and noting any speech problems (stuttering,
stammering, lisping). Also please note any language concerns, such
as decoding problems, mispronunciation, garbled sentences, or
suspected delayed reading skills that might interfere with students'
progress.

If you notice any of these conditions, please send the student's name
to me in Room 168 or place a notice in my mailbox. I will follow up
with the student and conduct a thorough screening. I appreciate your
assistance with this important task.

Body

- Explain the importance of the request.
- Give directions on how to comply.
- Describe any particular aspect that needs special attention. Model 3-25
  tells readers what to look for in student speech patterns.

Closing

- Remind the readers about deadlines.
- Express appreciation for the reader's help or emphasize the benefits
  resulting from the reader's help.
- State what you will do next.

(See also "Requests to Community Members" in Chapter 3.)

Responses to Requests from School Personnel

An internal response to a request may be a positive answer (you grant the request) or a negative one (you refuse the request). Whatever the answer, the memo should reflect the same courtesy that appears in a response letter sent to a parent or any member of the community.

Purpose

Most internal requests are based on teaching or service situations, and everyone shares the same goals—to enhance educational opportunities for district students. The response to a request should indicate that the writer or other authority seriously considered the reader's request. Avoid implying that the idea has no merit. Much school success derives from the collaborative efforts of educators who share goals and ideas in working to strengthen programs.

Organization

Internal responses to requests are in the direct organization pattern when the topic relates to an educational issue. If the topic is a personal one, such as a request from a secretary for special vacation time, a memo refusing the request might be written in the indirect organization pattern if the writer believes the reader will be upset at a refusal. Follow these guidelines:

Opening

- Identify the topic in the subject line and in the first paragraph.
- Express understanding of the request.
- State your answer to the request.

Body

- Explain the reasoning behind your answer. Model 3-26 explains how the writer wants to expand the original idea. The writer in Model 3-27 briefly states the reason for her refusal. She does not have to justify her refusal further.

Closing

- Indicate any necessary actions. The closing in Model 3-26 tells the reader how to submit expenses and directs him to contact the district office to expand the publicity effort.

MODEL 3–26   Positive Response to a Request Memo

To: Rick Donovan

From: Stephanie Borosky   *SB*
           Principal

Date: February 1, 1999

Re: Photography Expenses

Rick, I think your idea about video taping your fourth-grade class when poet Amy Cassetto visits on March 3 is a great one. We do have enough money in the special program budget to cover the taping and the still photography.

When I read your description of how Ms. Cassetto is planning to read her poems to the students and then look at the poetry books the students wrote, I realized that this event would be ideal for photography and community interest. The Communications Director at the district office might want to feature Ms. Cassetto's visit in a news release. Your photos will be useful for our newsletter and also for the district newsletter.

Go ahead and get the materials you asked for and submit the receipts with an expense form to Sonia in the office. Also, call Cindy Banton, Communication Director, in the district office at 555–5464 and find out about getting broader coverage of this event. This project is the kind that gives a real boost to our community image.

- Express goodwill, whatever your answer. The closing in Model 3-27 ends with a positive comment about the summer project.

Responses to requests are important documents because they have an impact on the personal confidence and enthusiasm of the person who wrote the request. Responses should support that feeling whether the answer to a request is yes or no. (See also "Responses to Requests from Community Members" in Chapter 3.)

Superintendent Update Memos to School Boards

A superintendent's update memo to the school board is a status report, providing information about the school district on a regular basis:

MODEL 3–27   **Negative Response to a Request Memo**

To: Dale Vandergert
            Principal

From: Lynne Kirakis   *Lynne*
            Sixth-Grade Teacher

Date: May 2, 1999

Re: Summer Open House

I was on the committee that developed new approaches to open house
activities for parents and guardians, and I think the idea of a
summer open house to acquaint parents and guardians with extra
learning opportunities is a wonderful idea. Much as I wish I could
participate, I will not be able to serve on the June/July committee
for the Summer Open House.

I am usually in town in the summer, as you mentioned, and in most
years I would be glad to serve. This summer, however, my husband
and I are taking a long-anticipated trip to visit his relatives in Athens
and will be gone during the summer program.

I expect this new initiative to interact with parents will be highly
successful, and I look forward to hearing about it when I return to
school.

---

weekly, twice a month, or whatever frequency is appropriate for the
school district. Generally, the superintendent of a district writes the
memo.

Purpose

The purpose of the update memo is to inform school board members of
recent events and alert them to issues that will arise at the next board
meeting. Include both positive and negative topics in the memo. News
about school achievements and successes creates positive public relations with the board members as they learn about the efforts of administrators, teachers, and staff to enhance student learning and support
district goals. Negative news should focus on how the issues or events
are being handled. If the issue is one that the board will have to discuss,
offer assistance or attach helpful materials, such as reports on the topic,

summaries of relevant legal decisions, or articles from educational journals to aid the board members in their deliberations.

Personnel matters, such as hiring, promotions, or negative performance reports, should be handled in separate correspondence. The update memo may be widely disseminated and is not the appropriate document in which to discuss personnel matters.

Organization

Organize an update memo by topic. Present each topic in a separate paragraph, and group topics under headings, such as "Achievements" or "Ongoing Building Repairs." The headings will guide board members to items of particular interest. Beginning the memo with district achievements presents good news before bad news and increases board members' confidence in the district activities. Follow these guidelines:

Opening

- Identify the exact time period covered in the memo.
- Because these memos constitute a series, some writers number them as well.
- Thank the board members for their interest and mention any significant feedback you received from the previous update memo. Model 3-28 opens by identifying the precise dates covered by the update memo.

Body

- Under each topic heading, begin with the item that you believe the board will find most interesting or that you believe is most important. The first achievement described in Model 3–28 is a grant to purchase teaching materials. Supplementary funds are always of interest to board members.
- Provide specific facts, such as dates, places, and names.
- If the topic is ongoing, summarize progress, explain any necessary change in deadlines, or highlight continued success.
- Identify teachers or staff who have contributed to a specific project's success or who have had a personal career success that reflects well on the district.
- Invite board members to participate in projects when appropriate. Model 3-28 asks board members if they wish to talk to the project manager of the school building renovations.

MODEL 3-28   Superintendent Update Memo to the School Board

To: District 67 Board Members
           John B. Anthos, Sarah S. Levine, Daniel V. McDermott,
           Jenelle M. Solari, Ai Leng Wong

From: Donald P. Johnston   *DPJ*
           Superintendent
           District 67

Date: November 16, 1999

Re: Update Report—School District 67

This review for November 12–16, 1999, includes exciting
achievements for our district. I appreciate your continued interest in
these updates and responses to ongoing concerns.

Achievements

Language teachers Jennifer Mayfield and Chet Archer, Winthrop
Middle School, were awarded a <u>Technology 2000 Pember Foundation
Grant of $1,000.</u> The grant provides funds to implement new
language study materials in the foreign language instruction in
grades six through eight.

Four Winthrop Middle School honor students submitted science
projects to the <u>State Science Fair</u> at Springfield, and all four were
accepted. Given the competition, this success for all four students is
exciting. The students will have special science block time to work on
the projects with faculty.

Central High School's Junior Reserve Officers' Training Corps
(JROTC) battalion has been named an <u>Honor Unit with Distinction</u> by
the Department of the Army for the 1999–2000 school year. This
honor is earned by battalions that demonstrate exceptionally high
standards of training and motivation.

Concerns

The attached copy of the <u>Tri-County Gazette</u>'s editorial (November 2,
1999) criticizes our transporting Winthrop Middle School students on
the same buses with Central High School students. I have written a
letter to the editor (copy attached) explaining that drivers monitor
student behavior carefully; middle school students sit directly behind
the driver. To date, we have had no difficulty with the arrangement.

(Continued)

MODEL 3–28   *Continued*

November 16, 1999   page 2

The issue of <u>inside suspension</u> remains troubling to some parents. I
have had two telephone calls this past week from parents who view
inside suspensions as "isolating" and "too severe." I explained that
the adult-supervised study time has proved to be quite effective in
helping students complete all their assigned homework and in
reinforcing the need for correct behavior in our schools. I have asked
Central High School Principal Theodore Orsini and Winthrop Middle
School Principal Robert Barr to report on the numbers of students
involved, especially "repeaters," since we began the program in
August 1998. I have also asked for counselor reports on students
involved.

I have received a letter from a local group, Supporters of Decent
Literature, asking for board meeting time to discuss removing "at
least ten books" from the library at Central High School. I will
duplicate several articles covering recent handling of objections to
library holdings and include them in your packet for the second
meeting this month. I will also include our district policy statement
on this issue.

Renovation Project

Renovations to four classrooms at Betsy Ross Elementary School are
still underway, and we continue to use the cafeteria for afternoon art
and music study. The project manager from Westside Construction
will meet with me next week. If you are interested in talking with
him, please let me know.

Future Projects

Jeannette Harris of Betsy Ross Elementary suggested that we print
a reference chart of important school telephone numbers for every
student's home. Parents would then have a handy list to use when
calling our district schools. I recommend that we refer this project to
the school PTAs and ask if they can take it on.

The Central High School PTA is asking for your ideas about a
monthly coffee hour, open to all interested school community
members, board members, administrators, and faculty. These coffee
hours would provide discussion time about district events,
curriculum, policies, and issues. I will place this item on the next
board agenda.

I am attending a conference November 18–20 in Springfield, but I will
be happy to discuss any of these matters when I am back in the
office.

- When reporting negative news, state what actions have been or will be taken to solve problems. If parents are concerned about an issue, tell board members how you have answered their questions.
- Attach relevant written materials that board members will need in order to understand a situation. The writer of Model 3-28 attaches a recent critical newspaper editorial, which board members may not have seen.
- If community members are demanding to speak to the board at the next meeting or demanding specific actions that violate district policy, attach relevant information about the matter. Or offer to speak to the board on the matter before the general meeting. Model 3-28 reports that a group is demanding removal of some library books. The writer attaches relevant information on this issue for board members.
- Explain any changes in items covered in previous memos.

Closing

- Preview any important topic coming up in the next update memo.
- Highlight any deadlines that demand attention.
- Invite readers to comment.
- Express willingness and availability to discuss topics.

Avoid Clipped Sentences

Do not omit articles, pronouns, or prepositions.

No: Wilson will hold planning meeting Thursday Hunter Lodge.

Yes: The Wilson High Faculty will hold its planning meeting on Thursday at Hunter Lodge.

4

Reports

Reports are documents that provide information to assist readers in decision making. Length can vary from one page to several hundred pages. The length of a report depends on how much information the reader needs to understand the situation. Reports frequently have multiple readers, and writers must include enough information to serve them all.

INFORMAL INTERNAL REPORTS

Purpose

The most common purposes for reports are the following:

- *To inform* readers about current school conditions or programs and activities, such as a report describing the deterioration of the school physical plant
- *To record* facts about programs, incidents, and decisions for future reference, such as a report giving school demographics, test scores, dropout rates, student–teacher ratios, and projected general fund budget
- *To recommend* specific actions to improve existing programs or handle current situations, such as a report recommending surveillance cameras
- *To persuade* readers that some action is needed in a controversial situation, such as a report arguing the need to close a school and demolish it

Before writing a report, analyze your reader, purpose, and situation as discussed in Chapter 1.

Most internal reports, whatever their purpose and length, are written in memo format. External reports are more often formal reports and include such elements as title page, transmittal letter, table of contents, list of tables and figures, and appendixes. (See "Guidance Reports," discussed later in this chapter.)

Organization

Internal and external reports, informal or formal, are organized in either a *direct organization* pattern with an opening summary or an *indirect organization* pattern with a delayed summary. Because educators are deluged with written material and need to understand information quickly, most reports are in the direct organization or opening-summary pattern. Writers use the indirect organization or delayed-summary pattern when they expect readers to resist the report information or conclusions.

Direct Organization

The direct organization pattern uses an opening summary that supplies the reader with essential information—the recommendation, conclusions, or results. With this opening, the reader understands the situation and the writer's position at once. This organization pattern has three main sections:

- *The opening summary* covers the subject of the report; special circumstances, such as deadlines or sources of information; main issues; conclusions, results, and recommendations. Busy readers, not directly involved in the subject, may rely on the opening summary to keep them informed about the situation. Readers who are involved rely on the opening summary to preview the contents and conclusions of the report. Model 4-1 illustrates the opening summary. The writers review the subject and recommend specific actions.
- *Data sections* provide the details and facts relevant to the report's purpose and the conclusions in the opening summary. In Model 4-1, the data sections explain the teachers' meetings, their concerns, and suggestions. Headings direct the reader to specific topics.
- *The closing* is another brief summary restating the conclusions, results, or recommendations. The closing may stress the importance of the subject or a pressing deadline. The writer may also offer to

MODEL 4–1   Report in Direct Organization Pattern

BEAVER SPRINGS MIDDLE SCHOOL
MEMORANDUM

To: Alan F. Morelli
           Principal

From: New Teachers Ad Hoc Committee   *KP*
           Kelly Prentice, Language Arts, Committee Chair

Date: November 3, 1999

Re: Extended Orientation Program for New Faculty

As you recall, during the August orientation period, we discussed
extending official mentoring and orientation through the first year.
The new teachers formed a committee to meet informally during the
first semester to discuss our teaching assignments and any questions
that might arise. We were to report to you at the end of the first
semester about our conclusions. At our latest meeting, we agreed
that we were ready now to suggest that orientation and mentoring
be extended through the first year for new teachers.

Weekly Meetings

The committee met eight times after the start of school, usually on
Thursday afternoons. Two of the meetings involved informal
presentations about teaching methods by Kathy Josephs and Debra
Paggett. These presentations were informative and much appreciated
by the new teachers.

Issues Raised in Meetings

As chair, I took notes on the issues committee members raised at our
meetings. Generally, a member described a current problem, and we
discussed options for handling it. I also kept a log of the types of
problems we encountered and solved through our discussions.
Following is the list of problems and the number involved during the
period August 27–October 31, 1999:

Telephone calls or meetings with parents	29
Community attitudes and feedback	7
Classroom discipline	16
Daily lesson plans	17

As motivated new teachers, we believe we have dealt successfully
with most of the issues, but we retain lingering concerns about
handling future problems effectively. For example, the following
incidents illustrate issues we are still uncertain about.

MODEL 4–1 *Continued*

Alan F. Morelli   -2-   November 3, 1999

- Cliff Buchanan reported last week that he gave a student a detention for roughhousing in the hallway during a passing period. The next day, he received a telephone call from the student's parent who said he had "no right to reprimand" her son.

- We are all concerned about lesson plans and how to adjust when the lessons do not proceed as expected.

Discussion has convinced us that there are issues about teaching and communicating with parents and the community that only experience can solve.

Suggested Mentoring Procedures

We ask that the New Teachers' Committee meet regularly with administrators for the remainder of the school year. We hope these meetings can include informal presentations by experienced faculty and staff and informal discussion of issues.

We also ask that you assign an experienced teacher as a mentor to each of the five new teachers. This personal mentor will be invaluable as a resource for answering daily questions.

Conclusion

Adding five newly certified teachers in one semester is unusual for our school, and we appreciate your concern about our transition to full-time teaching. We believe scheduling orientation meetings for the full year and assigning mentors will aid us in our commitment to excellence in teaching. If you would like to discuss this report, we would be glad to meet with you.

---

discuss the matter further or ask the reader for a decision or action. The conclusion in Model 4-1 repeats the writer's recommendations and offers to discuss the subject further.

The writer in Model 4-1 uses the direct organization pattern because the reader has asked for the report and knows some of the background of the subject.

Indirect Organization

The indirect organization has a delayed summary; the opening does not reveal the writer's recommendations or conclusions. Use the delayed summary when you believe the reader may resist your conclusions or your analysis of the situation. The indirect organization has three main sections:

- *The introductory paragraph* provides the same information as the opening summary, but does not include recommendations, results, or conclusions. Model 4-2 is a report with a delayed summary. The opening paragraph presents the subject, reminds the reader about the importance of the school football field, and establishes the problem, but does not include a recommendation.
- *Data sections* provide the relevant details about the subject. The writer in Model 4-2 reviews the details of the problem, explains why two potential solutions are not good choices, and then explains the best choice.
- *The closing* summarizes the main points, results, conclusions, and recommendations. This closing summary is essential because the reader needs to connect the data with the conclusions or recommendations. The closing summary in Model 4-2 repeats the recommendation for restructuring the football field. The writer also requests permission to present a formal proposal to the school board and offers to discuss the matter further.

The indirect organization pattern allows a writer to present data and a rationale before making a recommendation. Notice that the writer of Model 4-2 does not estimate the high cost of restructuring the football field. That cost will be in the proposal when board members will be more committed to the idea.

GUIDELINES AND MODELS
FOR SPECIAL REPORTS

The following are guidelines and models for types of reports that educators write frequently.

Academic Progress Report with Cover Letter

An academic progress report, or student progress report, is an academic and behavioral achievement assessment. The report, written by the appropriate teacher, is often a combination of a checklist evaluation and two or three paragraphs of narrative.

MODEL 4–2   Report in Indirect Organization Pattern

Date: June 1, 1999

To: Ethan W. Edwards
             Superintendent
             District 15

From: William C. Fields   *WCF*
             Principal
             Sam Houston High School

Re: Sam Houston High School Football Field

As you know, Sam Houston High School has won three architectural and four landscaping awards for public buildings and grounds, and we have always listed maintenance as a budget priority. Attendance at home football games has increased 6 percent since 1997, and attendance at our home soccer matches has increased 1.5 percent since 1998. To continue to attract good crowds at our athletic events and to maintain our reputation for attractive buildings and grounds, we need to consider ways to keep the football field in playing condition.

Problem

Although Hal Lloyd does an excellent job of regular maintenance, a continuing problem is that the crown of our field is not high enough. Drainage is very poor. Any significant rainfall creates a muddy field that players have to struggle with. Visiting coaches complain about conditions, and the Gazette often refers to our field as "the swamp." This kind of publicity does not enhance our community image.

Temporary Repairs

I asked Hal Lloyd to investigate possible repairs, and I have his year-end report. Resodding the field does not seem to be a good solution. Grass does not grow well on a field with a low crown because the poor drainage prevents good growth and ruins what grass does grow. Resodding would cost about $20,000 per 67,000 square feet, and I believe it would be a waste of money because of the likelihood that any growth would be temporary.

A second possibility would be to install artificial turf. Although turf would accommodate sports teams, band, and phys ed classes, this plan has two drawbacks. The cost would be very high, approximately $500,000. More important, research indicates that this hard surface may contribute to a higher incidence of injury than natural grass.

(Continued)

MODEL 4–2 *Continued*

Ethan W. Edwards
June 1, 1999
page 2

Restructuring the Field

The crown needs to be restructured and built up to improve drainage
and foster appropriate growing conditions for natural grass. This
restructuring will enhance the playing conditions for both football
and soccer; our competitors' opinions of our facilities will also
improve. Certainly, our players and coaches deserve the best field
we can give them for home games. If we act immediately, we should
have our field ready for league play when the fall 1999 season
begins.

Conclusion

Resodding or installing artificial turf are not the best solutions for
the current problem with our football field. Restructuring the crown
of the field is a permanent improvement in the playing conditions. If
you agree, I would like to prepare a formal proposal to present to the
board. I would include a preliminary analysis and cost estimate,
along with suggestions for involving the Booster Club and other
community supporters. I would be glad to discuss the matter in more
detail before going to the board.

Purpose
The academic progress report informs parents or guardians about a student's academic, behavioral, and social progress up to that date and
compares the student's work and skill level to the course goals and objectives. Parents receive these reports mid-quarter throughout the school
year. The narrative section is particularly important because readers are
most likely to depend on that for a clear assessment of the student's
progress and probable success or failure. In some elementary schools,
parent conferences may substitute for these academic reports in early
months of the academic year.

Organization
Organize the information by topic, so all discussion of the student's test
scores, for instance, is in one paragraph. Model 4-3 shows a cover letter
and sample narrative section of an academic progress report.

MODEL 4–3   Cover Letter and Narrative Section of Academic
Progress Report

Roosevelt High School
1500 S. Grant Parkway
Cleveland, OH 44239
(216) 555–6672

November 10, 1999

Dear Parent/Guardian:

Roosevelt High School is committed to helping all our students
achieve success in their schoolwork. Enclosed are one or more
academic progress reports written by teachers of your child. These
reports inform you about the specific achievements of your child in
a particular course. In addition, the reports indicate any areas that
require increased effort.

We believe parents can most effectively encourage and aid their
children if regular academic progress reports are available.

Teachers are always interested in meeting with you to discuss
homework, tests, and student progress. If you have questions about
these reports or your child's progress, please call teachers at 555–
6672 and make an appointment for a conference.

Sincerely,

Patrick C. Smith

Patrick C. Smith
Principal

Enc.

(Continued)

Opening

- Do not begin with negative information even if the report is mostly
  negative.
- Avoid blunt statements, such as "Bob is failing English." Also avoid
  beginning with information that may alienate the reader, such as
  "This is the first report since Marcy admitted cheating on a test."

MODEL 4–3 *Continued*

Narrative Section of Academic Progress Report

Matthew has good basic math skills and eagerly participates in classwork, often volunteering to write proofs on the board. I believe he has the ability to raise his grade average from the current 65 and maintain a C average in Geometry II. Because his two chapter test scores are below average, Matthew would fail the course if the grades were turned in now, but he has time to raise his average.

Matthew should complete every homework assignment because daily work on the problems will help him understand the material. He also needs to memorize formulas and principles so he can raise his quiz average. Any assistance that you can give toward making sure Matthew is spending time on his homework problems would help immensely.

I am concerned about the geometry project requirement, which counts as one-sixth of his final grade. Matthew has not come in to discuss his progress on the geodesic dome model and research study.

I am available every day before school (7 a.m. to 8 a.m.) and after school (3:30 p.m. to 4:00 p.m.) and would be glad to discuss Matthew's work with you. We have three more unit tests, several quizzes, daily homework, and participation scores this semester. I believe Matthew can achieve a solid passing grade if he focuses on his work.

- Begin with a positive statement about the student's ability or improvement since the last report. Notice that the first paragraph in the narrative section of Model 4-3 begins with a positive statement about the student's math ability and his class participation.

Paragraphs

- Focus on a specific topic. If necessary, explain why the student may receive a low grade on the next report card so parents are not surprised when report cards arrive.

- Base your overall evaluation of progress on specific information about the student's test and quiz scores, homework record, class participation, writing assignments, special projects, and group work.
- Identify specific areas in which the student needs to improve, such as completing homework assignments.
- Include suggestions for parents on ways to help their children study. Model 4-3 mentions homework and asks the parents to check that their child is completing assignments.
- If the information is negative, maintain a positive or neutral tone. Model 4-3 warns of possible failure but suggests the student has time to succeed in the course.

Closing

- Offer to discuss the student's progress.
- Suggest times for a conference.
- Preview the remaining tests, projects, and quizzes.

Parents can be upset by negative news in academic progress reports. Use these reports to stress the student's potential for success and to encourage parents to participate in the education process. A well-written academic progress report can be an effective public relations tool for your school. Because an academic progress report is a form with a narrative section and parents may receive several of these in one envelope, a brief cover letter should accompany these reports.

Cover Letter

The cover letter is a form letter on school letterhead addressed either individually or to "Dear Parent/Guardian." The letter, signed by the principal, is a courtesy to parents. Receiving several academic progress reports in an envelope may confuse parents, especially those new to the school system. Model 4-3 shows a typical cover letter.

Opening

- Identify the contents and purpose of the enclosures.
- Explain the purpose of the reports.

Body

- Stress the dedication of the school and faculty to improve student achievement.

Closing

- Suggest that the parents contact the school and ask questions.

The cover letter should reflect an interested school, administrators, and faculty. Use this important public relations opportunity to build understanding between parents and educators.

Convention Follow-up Reports

A convention follow-up report summarizes the individual presentations of speakers or panels at a specific convention.

Purpose

This report is a useful record for administrators, faculty, and staff who attended the convention and need a reminder about important topics. The report also informs school personnel who were not at the convention about the major convention topics. At some schools, convention attendees are expected to write a follow-up report for other faculty and staff; at all schools, writing such a report for others who are interested in the topics is a professional courtesy. Summarizing the entire convention schedule is usually not necessary. Always consider the needs of your particular readers and focus on the convention topics that are relevant to the issues facing your school or district.

Organization

Use the direct organization pattern. Follow these guidelines:

Opening

- Identify the official theme or slogan for the convention.
- State the full name of the organization, the inclusive dates of the meeting, and the exact location.
- Mention any prominent speakers, important keynote addresses, or significant resolutions at the meeting.
- Tell readers if you are summarizing topics in order of importance.

Model 4-4 is a convention follow-up report written by an assistant principal to the faculty and staff of a high school. The opening paragraph

MODEL 4–4   Convention Follow-up Report

To: Faculty and Staff
From: Michelle Ashland, Assistant Principal   *MA*
Date: January 10, 1998
Re: NAEP Conference

"Nonacademic Challenges—Ready or Not!" was the theme for the annual convention of the National Association of Educational Personnel held January 2–4, 1998, in Houston, Texas. Katharine Wiggins, Central Planning Administrator for Western State Schools, the keynote speaker, told the audience that they should not regard nonacademic problems as irritating interruptions in a busy day. She emphasized that solving these problems enhanced educational programs and improved the morale of the faculty, staff, and students. The following summary covers two topics that are especially important to the Randolph Park District.

Board/Staff Relations

Michael Chen, Franklin County, Ohio, board member, in a speech entitled "Creating Board/Staff Partnerships," called for increased communication and closer ties between school board members, faculty, and staff. Because of the commitment to site-based planning, Chen said members of a school system needed to understand all viewpoints on school issues, and he suggested several ways to increase communication:

1. Informal meetings between board members and staffs of district schools at luncheons, dinners, and coffees.
2. Regular departmental presentations at school board meetings, and inviting specific faculty and staff to board meetings.
3. Small-group problem-solving sessions where faculty, staff, and board members can address district issues with community leaders, parents, or other interested parties.

Chen reported great success in one Ohio district when they tried all these suggestions. The result was a united group of educational professionals, all committed to student success. Overall, Chen's presentation was a useful review of practical suggestions that could be tried here.

Parental/Guardian Involvement in Schools

Keisha McQueen, Superintendent of Milwaukee County Public Schools, spoke on "How Much Parental Involvement Is Too Much?" She urged the audience to set up specific guidelines for stakeholders'

(Continued)

MODEL 4–4 *Continued*

Faculty and Staff   -2-   January 10, 1998

involvement in local educational efforts and described several
problems that can arise as districts use participatory management
and site-based planning. One issue involves committee work and
members who believe their decisions will be immediately
implemented. Committee members often have difficulty
understanding the advisory role of school committees.

Another conflict arises when parents believe they can interrupt the
school day whenever they wish. McQueen mentioned one suburban
high school that had a problem with parents who simply showed up
in the building, walked around, and entered classes unannounced.
Another example of "overinvolvement" occurred in a Milwaukee
school when the mother of a student participating in the spring play
decided to attend a rehearsal and announced, "We can make this play
professional. I was once on the stage and can come to every
rehearsal and help direct." The mother attended many rehearsals,
suggesting "improvements," and often attempted to overrule the
drama coach. Students were uncomfortable and not sure how to
respond to the mother.

This presentation was an effective warning about parental
overinvolvement. McQueen's guidelines included the following:

1. Explain the necessary parameters of involvement in school
   affairs.
2. Acknowledge the crucial need for stakeholders' input.
3. Ask the superintendent or a board member to explain how
   "final decisions" are made in the district.

Conclusion

Overall, the convention speakers suggested establishing district
communication guidelines and a clear communication policy. Other
topics covered were communicating with architects and construction
specialists about adapting school buildings for new learning
opportunities, school bus safety, and developing strict building
maintenance schedules. I have extra copies of the convention
program in my office.

identifies the keynote speaker, a prominent educator, to emphasize the
convention's theme. The writer directs readers to the two specific topics
summarized in the report.

Information Sections

The information sections should highlight specific topics. If possible, cover the topics in descending order of importance.

- Use headings with key words to guide the reader to specific topics.
- State the full name and title or affiliation of each speaker you mention, as well as the full title of the presentation. If you do not have the title, state the overall subject of the presentation.
- Avoid general statements, such as "The speaker discussed many problems." Be specific: "The speaker cited three reasons for decreasing parental involvement."
- Do not summarize everything the speaker said; focus on the main points.
- Conclude each section with a statement of the overall importance or usefulness of the speaker's presentation.

The writer in Model 4-4 uses key words in headings to attract reader attention to topics. The sections have sufficient detail for readers to understand the main ideas of the presentations.

Closing

The conclusion should be brief.

- Mention other topics covered in convention sessions and your willingness to share information about them.
- Offer to discuss the major topics in your report with interested personnel.
- Remind readers about any particularly relevant information that directly affects your school or district.

The Model 4-4 writer briefly mentions other topics discussed at the convention and offers to discuss them further.

Educators exchange important information about academic and nonacademic issues at conventions. A convention follow-up report helps disseminate the information beyond those who attended the convention and increases professional development for readers.

Guidance Reports

The term *guidance report* covers a variety of documents. Guidance reports, in general, provide records of students and their academic, disciplinary, and personal issues.

Guidance personnel at elementary, middle school, and high school keep formal and informal reports on all subjects concerning students, such as records of meetings with teachers, parents, and students; student–peer relationships; social interactions, and advisory and referral reports on students. These reports may go to parents, administrators, state board of education personnel, and support service agencies. Guidance coordinators may also write formal reports that evaluate the progress and success of large support programs, either experimental or ongoing.

Purpose

Guidance reports vary in content, form, and special purpose, but they are all concerned with recording specific information about individual students, groups of students, and select programs for students classified as at risk, underachieving, or gifted and talented.

Internal Guidance Report

Model 4-5 is an internal guidance report of a counselor's meeting about an underachieving student. The meeting involved the student's parent, teachers, and advisor. Some schools have established forms for internal guidance reports. If no such form exists, follow these guidelines:

Heading

- Identify the student involved, grade level, the date of the report, and the names and positions of everyone in attendance.
- List anyone who should have participated but was not able to attend.
- Record the general purpose of the meeting and the date of the meeting. Reports are usually written soon after such a meeting, but the date of the report and the date of the meeting may differ; record both.

Body

- Record relevant discussion and decisions about goals and follow-up plans for helping the student.
- Use headings, such as discussion, goal, follow-up plan, and possible future interventions. These headings help readers find specific areas that they expect to see in such a report. Major sections may be divided into subtopics, as is the discussion section in Model 4-5.

Closing

- Summarize the problem and plans for helping the student.
- Mention any scheduled meetings.

MODEL 4–5   Student Guidance Report

Report of Guidance Meeting on Jill Chandler

Date: February 12, 1999
Student: Jill Chandler
Grade Level: 9 (Homeroom 120)
Advisor: Bernice Tomlinson
Guidance Counselor: Angela Whatley

Present: Mrs. Marjorie Chandler, parent; Mrs. Angela Whatley, counselor; Mrs. Bernice Tomlinson, homeroom advisor; Mr. Peter Craik, Algebra I; Ms. Natalie Delotte, French; Mr. Mark Ferguson, Computer Science; Ms. Janet Webster, English; Ms. Rosa Diaz, Physical Education; Mr. Michael Withers, Biology I

Absent: Mr. Sam Wynegate, Social Studies I

Purpose: This report reviews the Guidance meeting on February 11, 1999, on Jill Chandler

Discussion:

Parental Concern: Mrs. Chandler requested the meeting because she is concerned about Jill's lack of interest in school and her lack of homework. When Mrs. Chandler questions Jill, her daughter says she does her homework "at school in study hall."

Student's Current Status: Jill's mid-quarter reports will have low overall averages in algebra and French. She is "borderline passing" in English, pending a unit test, and she will receive a warning of a potential failing grade for biology on the mid-quarter report. Her computer science and social studies grades are in the 75 percent range.

Faculty Observations: Mr. Craik reported a poor effort in algebra; Ms. Delotte said Jill made no attempt to participate in group practice in French. Ms. Diaz noted that Jill told her she did not like physical education, and she held back when forming teams. Mr. Ferguson said Jill seems to enjoy the computer units; however, she is not turning in homework. Ms. Webster said Jill could do better in English, but her lack of homework was contributing to her low grades on quizzes. In his absence, Mr. Wynegate forwarded Jill's grades in social studies, indicating an average of 75 percent. Mr. Withers said Jill's grades in biology also were at the 75 percent level. Homeroom advisor Bernice Tomlinson said she was unaware of any achievement problems in her talks with Jill.

Overall Assessment: Jill's incoming test scores showed above-average ability with no indication she would have difficulty achieving. First semester grades showed average achievement in all subjects. Jill shows no evidence of anxiety, drugs, gang membership,

(Continued)

MODEL 4–5 *Continued*

Report of Guidance Meeting on Jill Clandler, p, 2

or general rebellion. All present agreed that Jill should be achieving at least 80 percent in her classes. After her teachers reviewed Jill's progress, Mrs. Chandler said her daughter spent last summer in California with relatives and now has "unrealistic expectations" about relocating.

Goal:

All present agreed that Jill should raise her current grade average and develop achievement priorities. Her coursework and completion of homework assignments should be the first concern. Mrs. Whatley will meet with Mrs. Chandler and Jill to explore Jill's wish to live in California.

Follow-up Plan:

All teachers present agreed to conference with Jill to discuss her coursework, her attitude, and how to improve her grades. Mr. Wynegate will be asked to do the same. Jill will have tutorials for each subject twice a week until she has significant improvement.

Jill will carry a "Weekly Academic Report" for teachers to fill out. Mrs. Chandler will receive one copy; the other will go to Mrs. Whatley in the guidance office. Teachers may phone Mrs. Chandler to discuss special concerns or Jill's progress.

Possible Future Interventions:

If no significant progress is made within one month of this meeting, the following may be implemented:

- Weekly meetings with counselor
- Additional tutorials
- Weekly conferences between Mrs. Chandler and Mrs. Whatley
- Referral to special support staff as indicated

Summary:

Jill Chandler is not achieving academically. Her mother and teachers are concerned about lower than expected grades, which may be related to Jill's expressed desire to live in California. Jill will be encouraged to explore the realities of relocation as she works on raising her grades. Teachers will review her progress with her weekly. After discussions about the unlikelihood of moving to California, Jill may realize her need to set new academic goals.

Next Meeting: February 26, 1999

External Formal Report

Model 4-6 is an external formal report from a guidance program coordi-nator of the regional supervisor of the state board of education. This for-mal report includes a transmittal letter and title page and presents information under specific headings. Whatever the subject, three sec-tions should appear in a formal report:

Introduction. This section should establish the purpose of the report and identify relevant programs, schools, and personnel. If appropriate, the introduction can also include the overall conclusion: "This program has been successful in reducing dropout rates 32 percent." If the report is lengthy, the introduction may also preview the contents: "This report covers planning, testing, and evaluating."

Recommendations. List recommendations under a separate heading. Even if recommendations appear throughout the report, gather them under one heading at the end of the report as a convenience to readers.

Conclusion. The conclusion of a formal report summarizes the major points in the report and repeats significant results. The conclusion may also suggest future actions or request further discussion. Do not include new information in the conclusion, but do mention scheduled meetings or future progress reports. Notice that the conclusion in Model 4-6 men-tions summer planning meetings scheduled over three months.

Other traditional features of external formal reports include the transmittal letter and a title page.

Transmittal Letter

A *transmittal letter* accompanies the report to the person who officially receives the report. The letter covers items that do not fit readily in the formal report.

- State the report title and indicate that the report is enclosed or attached.
- Establish the purpose of the report.
- Identify any state program, law, or code that is relevant to the report.
- Summarize briefly the major subject of the report.
- Point out any particularly relevant data in the report.
- Acknowledge those who participated in writing the report or who contributed specific data.
- Mention any planned follow-up reports or future study.
- Offer to provide more information or discuss the subject.

MODEL 4-6   Formal Report on Guidance Program

School District 17
Eisenhower High School
700 N. Ocean Drive
San Marcos Beach, California 92066
(818) 555-1333

June 4, 1999

Ms. Evelyn L. Herewood
Southern California Regional Supervisor
California Board of Education Services
200 S. Central Avenue
Mission View, CA 93964

Dear Ms. Herewood:

Enclosed is Eisenhower High School's report on the second year of a
three-year pilot program to meet the state board priority "Focus on
Graduation." The enclosed report fulfills state Special Program
guidelines requiring submission of reports on or before the
conclusion of the regular academic year.

We initiated the program to deal with our school's steadily rising
dropout rates. As you may recall, our program targets average to
above-average students who do not have a record of disciplinary
problems. Guidance Counselor Angela Whatkin assisted me in
gathering information for this report.

Please let me know if you would like copies of all records, including
minutes of planning meetings. Charts of demographic trends are also
available. Best wishes for a productive summer. I look forward to
seeing you at the conference in Atlanta in July.

Sincerely,

Alexander Campbell

Alexander Campbell
EES Program Coordinator

Enclosure

MODEL 4–6   *Continued*

Second Year Report on

Education Equals Success Program

School District 17

Eisenhower High School

Prepared for
Evelyn L. Herewood
Southern California Regional Supervisor
California Board of Education Services

Prepared by
Alexander Campbell
EES Program Coordinator
School District 17
Eisenhower High School

May 30, 1999

(Continued)

MODEL 4–6 *Continued*

Second Year Report On
Education Equals Success
School District 17—Eisenhower High School

Introduction

This report describes the goals and progress of the Education Equals Success (EES) program for the academic year 1998–1999, the second year of the program at Eisenhower High School, School District 17. The program began a three-year trial in the 1997–1998 academic year.

Purpose

The EES program focuses on Eisenhower High School students in grades 9–12 who are at risk for dropping out of school before graduation. The targeted students do not have a history of behavior and/or discipline problems. However, these students do reflect lower academic achievement than their average or above-average test scores indicate. The test batteries do not reveal any need for individualized services. The EES program is a response to the slow but steady rise in nongraduating students in this school district.

Description of Program

EES provides Eisenhower High School students with individualized attention, so they can achieve the academic success appropriate to their abilities. The long-range goal is to retain the students in the school system, so they can graduate with their respective classes. Following is the general chronology of EES actions for each student.

1. Identify students at risk through test scores, grades, staff recommendations, or parent input.

2. Meet with student; assess problems.

3. Schedule student guidance meeting with parent/guardian, advisor, counselor, and teachers.

4. Suggest interventions, such as tutorials, before, during, and after school; elective individualized "Study Skills" mini-course; upper-class peer as "buddy"; appointment with social worker or psychologist; exchange of study hall time with subject area laboratory or resource center attendance;

MODEL 4–6 *Continued*

Reports on EES   -2-   May 30, 1999
Eisenhower High School

    alternate time or help in other classes with identical subject
matter.

5. Meet with student, counselor, and advisor.

6. Monitor student progress.

7. Determine student's nonacademic areas of interests and
   skills; if relevant, incorporate job shadowing or an
   internship.

8. Reinforce weekly successes.

9. Involve parents in follow-up at home discussing appropriate
   study habits; reviewing course requirements; scheduling
   work sessions.

10. Send positive academic progress reports home.

11. Individualize the student's next course load, choosing a
    schedule and courses that meet the student's needs.

Current Program in Progress

The Eisenhower EES program at the end of its second year includes
22 at-risk students (five 9th graders; six 10th graders; four 11th
graders; seven 12th graders). Overall, 81.5 percent of participating
students have raised achievement levels at least one grade in each
subject this year. The remaining 18.5 percent required additional,
external community resource and support services. After receiving
the services, these students achieved nearly identical gains to the
other students at three, five, and seven weeks.

Teachers support EES and accommodate the students' learning styles
with tutorials, taped class discussions, special test reviews,
specialized worksheets, and supplementary textbooks. Teachers
focus on positive achievements, rather than on deficiencies, in the
academic progress reports.

Other students are aware of EES, and an informal sampling of ten
homerooms indicates that the students in general perceive the
program very positively, as do the parents.

(Continued)

MODEL 4–6 *Continued*

Reports on EES   -3-   May 30, 1999
Eisenhower High School

The Guidance Department budget funded this year's EES "Effort Awards," given at a special in-school meeting. The awards included gift certificates for a local book and music store.

Program Success

At the end of its second year, the EES program at Eisenhower High School continues to garner parent and community interest and approval. Students involved express their appreciation of individualized attention, especially from an advisor they can consult about academic, social, and personal problems. Teachers, parents, and students are pleased with increased involvement in classes and resulting higher grade averages.

The EES program works well because it models a "school-within-a-school" structure. The central location of the Guidance Department allows a "home base" for participating students, who gather at least twice a day in the conference room to compare workloads, talk about their interests, or make appointments to see advisors and counselors. EES students are responding positively by supporting and encouraging each other.

No student at Eisenhower High School has dropped out of the EES program during its first two years.

Overall Recommendation

The EES program should continue at Eisenhower High School and incorporate all the students who need help reaching graduation. As the community demographics of Eisenhower High School continue to change, increased numbers of students need individualized attention. One of the goals in the "Ideals for Schools" document of the State Board of Education, supported by District 17, is to reach greater numbers of students with problems, helping them achieve academic success leading to graduation. All those involved with the EES program believe that it is a highly successful way of supporting that goal.

Specific Recommendations

Following are some recommendations for specific actions to enhance the EES program in its third year.

MODEL 4–6 *Continued*

Reports on EES   -4-   May 30, 1999
Eisenhower High School

1. Plan a series of field trips to vocational, community college, and university sites.

2. Involve community resources more effectively by including local industrial and business sites offering shadowing and internships, as well as the state park system with volunteer and summer work.

3. Create a core group of advisors trained in the program requirements through summer workshops led by EES staff. New or potential advisors will mentor students and supervise EES small-group student discussions for a semester before full-time program involvement.

4. Create a committee representing parents/guardians, board members, administrators, and department chairs to evaluate, refine, and test EES efforts.

5. Consider options designed to lighten course and counseling loads of advisors and counselors.

6. Increase conference room space. Original planning did not anticipate the frequent meetings and socializing among these students—a positive outcome that should be encouraged.

7. Analyze how greater numbers of EES students can be accommodated.

Conclusion

EES has been a successful response to high dropout rates of Eisenhower High School students who have the ability to fulfill academic requirements for graduation. The program meets the needs of these students and gives them a select peer group whose members reinforce positive change. Teachers, counselors, parents, and students all value the program. There is interest in expanding the program if resources are available.

Guidance personnel anticipate a highly successful 1999–2000 school year. Planning meetings are scheduled once a month for June, July, and August. The meetings will focus on informal sharing of strategies and concerns about refining and enhancing the program.

Title Page.   The *title page* of a formal report records the report title, writer, reader, and date of the report. The title page may appear before the transmittal letter, but more often it follows the transmittal letter and includes the following elements:

- Title of the report, centered in the top third of the page. The title of the report should accurately reflect the contents and instantly tell a reader what the subject is. Do not use abbreviations in the title of a report.
- Name, title, and school or district of the person who receives the report, centered in the middle of the page.
- Name, title, and school or district of the writer, centered in the bottom third of the page.
- Date of the report, centered two to four lines under the writer's name.

A long formal report may also require a *table of contents* if the material is presented in chapters. If the report includes tables or figures, such as bar charts, line graphs, pie charts, or maps, a *list of illustrations* is necessary to guide readers to specific data. Follow these guidelines for a list of illustrations:

- List tables together; list figures together.
- Place the list of figures first in the list of illustrations, followed by the list of tables.
- Title each table and figure: "Spring 1998 Enrollment" or "Map of Bridgeport Student Populations."
- Number tables and figures consecutively. Number tables separately from figures: "Table 6, Student Conference Hours, and Figure 3, SAT Scores, show our improvement in these areas."
- Refer to the table or figure by number in the report: "The scores shown in Table 4 are from the first year. Figure 2 shows the comparison of two years."

Some formal reports also require appendixes of information, such as copies of surveys, interview transcriptions, statistical results, and case histories. Label each with a specific name and number or letter: "Appendix A: Survey Results."

Personnel Evaluation Reports

An evaluation report, also called a performance appraisal or personnel evaluation, is a record of a supervisor's assessment of how well the educator or noncertified staff member is performing on the job. The methods of evaluating certified and noncertified personnel vary greatly. Large public school systems usually have formal evaluation procedures, often based on union contracts, that determine the type of evaluation, the categories of review, and the acceptable terms for the review. A private academy may have an informal evaluation system based on an annual talk with the employee.

The evaluation report usually is a form report. It consists of (1) a checklist of the duties or expectations for the position, such as "maintains good discipline" or "uses appropriate telephone manner," and (2) a narrative section completed by the supervisor, such as the principal, or the team coordinator if the appraisal is done by a group. Both the evaluator and the employee sign the finished report; copies are usually filed in the district office.

Purpose

The evaluation report should serve the administrative and legal needs of the institution and also motivate the employee to improve or to continue to excel. An institution needs a detailed assessment of an employee's performance to support decisions on rehiring, salary adjustments, remediation, or termination. Employees are entitled to know how the supervisor perceives their strengths and weaknesses.

Because the evaluation report is based on the job description for a position, certified and noncertified employees are evaluated under different criteria. The form report with a checklist saves time and ensures that all employees in a particular category are evaluated according to the same factors. The narrative section of the report allows the writer to present a more individualized picture of the employee's work than is possible with a checklist.

Organization

The performance evaluation form is usually written to accommodate union contract requirements and the performance standards dictated by the job description. Forms should always contain adequate identification factors: school, district, employee, job title, date of report, date of observation or interview, class observed, and type of evaluation, such as

"Observation and Evaluation." Evaluation forms may also include a statement of goals for the evaluation and an explanation of the rating system used for the checklist.

> **Checklists**—The checklist for certified employees covers teaching strategies: "knows subject area" or "maintains good discipline." A separate checklist covers professional responsibilities: "duty assignment participation" or "coach or club/activity advisor." The checklist for noncertified employees covers job responsibilities: "works well with others" or "prioritizes daily tasks." The factors in the checklists are rated according to an established numerical standard, such as "2—performs above standard level." If there is no numerical standard, the factors usually are rated "meets expectations," "exceeds expectations," or "needs improvement."
>
> **Narrative sections**—The narrative sections provide the most valuable information in an evaluation because the writer can explain observations, describe specific behaviors, relate actions to institutional goals, and add pertinent information not covered in the checklists.
>
> * Avoid generalities: "Students were unruly."
> * State facts: "Students threw pencils and paper wads."
> * Clearly label your opinions: "I believe" or "I think."
> * Include positive as well as negative points.
> * Begin with positive points so negative factors do not overshadow the positive.
> * Make specific suggestions for improvement.

Model 4-7 shows the narrative sections in an evaluation report for a first-year teacher. The first section comments on the classroom observation, describing the teacher's method and the behavior of the students. The writer emphasizes the teacher's preparation, but reveals that his methods are not effective in holding students' attention or in meeting the district's goals for student involvement. The second section suggests the teacher use his coaching skills to create group learning and involve students. The overall recommendation summarizes both the teacher's strengths and his weaknesses and repeats the suggestion that he increase student involvement. The writer also comments on the teacher's strengths. These sections identify specific areas for improvement and suggest new approaches.

MODEL 4–7   Narrative Sections of a Teacher Evaluation Report

Comments Regarding Class Observation

Mike had a specific goal for this class period: Students will understand and provide definitions for the terms natural resources, climate, environment, and geographic factors. This goal fits curriculum standards. Mike's written lesson plans are always detailed and organized. One district goal is to involve students in a lesson through technological applications or other supplemental materials. Mike presented information entirely through lecture. I believe students paid attention because I was in the room. As I left, students began talking, and their shouts could be heard in the hallway within a few minutes. Although Mike managed and directed the class lesson, he did not fully involve students in the learning process.

Additional Comments Regarding Professional Responsibilities

Mike is a superb basketball coach who expects great effort from his junior team members. He needs to convey those same expectations to students in his third-period class. Our students must assume some responsibility for their own learning, but they cannot be expected to listen to lectures for a long period of time. With his basketball players, Mike creates practice groups, and each group reinforces its members. The same strategy could be used to engage students in group learning and increase their interest and involvement. I also suggest he involve parents in their child's progress, especially for the students who misbehave or are inattentive.

Overall Recommendation

Mike is a new teacher who is motivated and a meticulous recordkeeper. Currently, he manages his class by speaking in a loud tone and threatening additional assignments. However, he says that he does not always follow through with these assignments. His physical presence silences some students when he approaches their desks. Mike needs to practice getting students involved in the lesson through group activities. I believe his coaching skills can transfer to the classroom.

Evaluation reports can seriously affect a person's career and may constitute legal evidence under certain circumstances. Choose your words carefully.

Recommendation Reports

A recommendation report describes a need or problem and suggests specific actions to fulfill the need or solve the problem. The report may be written by noncertified staff, teachers, counselors, or administrators and is addressed to the person who is the immediate superior of the writer. Because several people may have to read the report before anyone makes a decision about the recommendation, the writer must take this wide readership into account when describing the situation and suggesting solutions. Recommendation reports sometimes appear as formal reports.

Purpose

Recommendation reports may be either solicited (the reader asked for the report and is expecting it) or unsolicited (the reader does not expect the report). If the recommendation report is unsolicited, the writer must consider whether the reader is likely to agree that there is a problem. The writer may need to convince the reader that a need or problem exists before presenting the recommendation. The overall purpose of all recommendation reports is to persuade the reader that the writer has interpreted the situation correctly and is recommending the appropriate solution.

Recommendation reports must emphasize the importance or urgency of the situation and the benefits to the school and students if the recommended action is taken. The writer also needs to consider, if possible, how the reader will react. Will the reader react favorably or negatively to the recommendation? If you believe your reader will react negatively, include more persuasive information, such as which schools are already using your idea or the discussion of the topic at a recent educational conference.

Organization

Because your purpose is to persuade the reader to accept your ideas, organize your report as a problem–solution document, so your reader understands the situation as you do. Follow these guidelines:

Subject line

- State that you are making a recommendation about a specific subject. Model 4-8 contains a long subject line that identifies the name of the grant and the focus of the recommendation—expenditures.

Opening Summary

- Describe the need or problem clearly.
- Explain why action is needed now.
- Explain how the situation affects student learning or district goals.
- If the problem is an old one, point out when it began, and mention any previous decisions about handling it.
- State any deadlines for taking action.
- Identify special sources, such as government reports or a survey.
- Briefly summarize the recommendation or state that you are recommending several actions.

The opening summary in Model 4-8 reminds the reader about the grant terms and says the writers have several recommendations for spending the remaining money.

Description of Recommendation

The headings in this section should identify your recommendation. The Model 4-8 headings identify specific items being recommended.

- Describe precisely what you are recommending.
- Explain any special circumstances, such as phase-in of your idea.
- Explain any timetable for actions.
- Describe any equipment you want to purchase.
- Describe any proposed changes in present systems.
- Mention any district mandates to take the action you recommend.
- If costs are complicated, break down the total to individual costs and provide a budget.
- Explain how to evaluate your plan, if relevant.
- Emphasize the expected benefits. If you expect resistance to your recommendation, emphasize benefits by putting them in a separate section called "Expected Benefits," and describe them one at a time.
- Show how the school need or problem will be solved.

MODEL 4–8   Recommendation Report

To: Ronald Pergrand
             Principal

From: Rachel Segal, Chemistry   *RS*
             Michael Mikoski, Biology   *MM*

Date: August 27, 1999

Re: Recommendation for State Science Curriculum
             Development Grant Expenditures

Opening Summary

We are entering the second and final year of the State Science
Curriculum Development Grant with $2,500 available for
expenditures this year. In the first year of the grant, we spent
$3,500 of the total $6,000 available. The grant specifically states
that we must spend approximately half of the money in each of the
two years. We have consulted informally with other teachers and our
librarian about our progress in bolstering our science programs. To
make the best use of our remaining funds, we are recommending the
following use of the money.

Expand Library Holdings of Science CD-ROMs

Presently, we have no physical science CD-ROMs. We very much need
new computer materials focused on the physical sciences. These new
materials will provide ample opportunity for student-centered
learning with interactive features. Following are the items we are
recommending for purchase.

- Weather Events—This CD-ROM covers the development of the
  major weather events, such as blizzards, floods, hurricanes,
  tornadoes. Also included are an interactive weather
  forecasting program and coverage of pollution, the greenhouse
  effect, and El Niño patterns.
- Mysteries of Oceanography—This CD-ROM explores the
  oceans, covering surface flow, swell and turbulence, and the
  ocean floors. It includes a unit on underwater archaeological
  mapping and searching for artifacts, which might be useful in
  social science classes.
- Biology of Plants and Animals—This CD-ROM (a set of four
  disks) covers the full range of principles in plant and animal

MODEL 4–8 *Continued*

Ronald Pergrand   -2-   August 27, 1999

life and includes an interactive unit on Darwin's travels and discovery of evolutionary evidence.

- DNA and Genetics—This CD-ROM covers DNA testing, blood typing, and genetics testing with various interactive units. Included is a unit on the ethics of testing.

We have the purchasing information for these CD-ROMs; they total about $1,100.

In-Service Training

Because we have one teacher this year who has not taught science in seven years and several teachers who have not used computer materials for long units, we recommend a one-day in-service session. This training can be scheduled during the Christmas break so teachers are ready to use the new materials when school resumes in January. There are nine physical science teachers. At a rate of $100 per teacher for a 6-hour session, total expenditure is $900.

Library Books

We recommend a review of library resources for physical science classes. The review should reveal areas that we need to build up. We recommend purchasing needed library books with the remaining $500 of the grant.

Conclusion/Recommendations

Changes in science come rapidly, and our students must have the most recent materials in order to prepare appropriately for college work. The guidance report in June 1999 indicated that 83 percent of Lewis and Clark High School students go on to college and 47 percent of that number are planning to major in a science. That number is an indication of how important our science curriculum is to our students. We recommend purchase of the CD-ROMs, training for the science teachers, and purchase of science books for the library out of the remaining funds in the State Science Curriculum Development Grant.

Conclusion and Recommendations

Readers pay the most attention to the openings and closings of reports, so your final section must repeat your recommendation and emphasize the benefits as strongly as possible.

- Summarize the seriousness of the problem or the compelling need.
- Restate your recommendation without the details.
- Summarize the major benefits from your recommendation.
- Mention any district, state, or federal guidelines.

The closing in Model 4-8 reminds the reader that the school has a high percentage of students interested in science and they need up-to-date materials to prepare for college.

(See also "Persuasive Messages" in Chapter 2.)

Avoid Artificial Language

Do not use language that is pretentious, old-fashioned, or more difficult to understand than necessary. Artificial language slows down readers.

No: Attached herewith is the compilation detailing student accelerating test scores for the biannual.

Yes: Attached is the annual report showing higher student test scores over the past six months.

5

News Messages to the Community

Because schools provide an essential service, parents and other community members have a natural interest in what happens in them. Administrators often write messages for the community at large, explaining new programs, goals, and events. These news messages keep interested people informed about their schools. Announcements, press releases, and newsletters describe events, activities, and new programs. Other messages for the public, such as mission statements and policies and procedures, explain the goals of the institution and the decisions educators have made to support these goals. Whatever the topic, every news message is an opportunity to enhance the image of the school and explain the principles guiding educational programs. This chapter covers some of the most common news messages educators write.

ANNOUNCEMENTS AND FLYERS

A flyer is a one-page announcement of a topic that interests several different groups. Usually, the topic is a broad one that affects many students, parents/guardians, and community members. A flyer is not appropriate for an announcement about a topic that affects a limited number of students or that applies only to special circumstances. (See also "Information Letters to Parents/Guardians" and "Announcements to School Personnel" in Chapter 3.)

Purpose
Flyers usually announce events that all interested parties may attend. Typical subjects are general meetings, public auctions of used equipment, benefits for school-related projects, homecoming parade route, athletic competitions, stadium parking and regulations, athletic team pep rallies, and school plays and activities for which the public may purchase tickets. The primary purpose of a flyer is to announce the event and provide basic information about time, date, place, tickets, and parking, including any restrictions.

Flyers are distributed in several ways. Students can bring them home, or they may be mailed or handed out in crowded places such as shopping areas. Area stores may allow school flyers in their windows, and flyers usually are placed on all appropriate bulletin boards.

Organization
Because flyers are distributed so broadly and are read while they hang on bulletin boards, one page is the best length for an effective announcement. Any size paper can be used, but you might have difficulty finding space on bulletin boards or in windows if your flyer is very large. A standard piece of typing paper is the most useful size. You may write the announcement with the longest side of the paper in either a horizontal or a vertical direction.

A school's announcement should be eye-catching but not gimmicky. The flyer is an informational document that represents the school's administrators and faculty even if the authors appear to be students. No matter how you format the announcement, include the following information:

- Identify the exact event being announced.
- Use formal titles, full names, exact locations.
- Provide exact times (with A.M. and P.M.), full dates, locations, and topics if the event is a meeting.
- Identify the purpose of the event.
- Identify any well-known speaker.
- Explain the event schedule if it is not obvious.
- Mention any deadlines, special rules, and ticket prices, if relevant.
- Conclude with a "call to action" persuading readers to participate in the event.
- Use a pleasant tone with "you-attitude."

The flyer in Model 5-1 has a descriptive heading followed by an intriguing question to catch reader attention. The flyer lists sample discussion topics to interest readers. The closing invites readers to the town meetings.

MODEL 5–1   Flyer

TOWN MEETINGS ON SCHOOLS AND EDUCATION

Black River High School	Custer Middle School
Pioneer Elementary School	Riverside Elementary School

Can You Spare Four Evenings During The Coming School Year To Discuss Current Education Issues With School Administrators, Faculty, Coaches, And Staff?

Black River School District 112 invites all community members interested in our public education system and our schools to join us in four Town Meetings to discuss these educational issues:

- **Discipline**
- **Safety**
- **Citizenship Education Program**
- **State Proficiency Tests**
- **Basic Skills Curriculum**
- **Student Service Requirements**
- **Your concerns and any other topic of interest**

Representatives of all District 112 schools will be on hand to explore the issues with you.

DATES:	**Monday, August 2, 1999**
	Monday, November 4, 1999
	Monday, February 3, 2000
	Monday, May 6, 2000
TIME:	**7:00 p.m. to 9:00 p.m.**
PLACE:	**McKinley Auditorium**
	Black River High School
	670 Summit Drive
MODERATOR:	**Michael Maloney, Board President**

Strong schools build strong communities. Please join us for one or all of these important meetings. Bring your questions, comments, opinions, and suggestions.

Format

Flyer format can vary with your purpose and audience. Consider these factors in designing your flyer.

Type. Readers may see your flyer in windows or on bulletin boards, so you must consider reading distance.

- Use type about one-half inch high for the heading. The heading should be legible at least five feet away to attract readers and entice them to pause and read the rest of the announcement.
- Use 10- or 12-point type for the text. The body of the flyer should be easy to read while someone is standing about two feet from the bulletin board.
- Use both capitals and lowercase letters for the text. This combination is more readable than all capitals or all lowercase letters.
- Do not use italics in a flyer. They are difficult to read.
- Use boldface for headings or to emphasize times, dates, locations, and other items you want readers to notice.

Text. The text should be easy to read, should emphasize important information, and should be arranged so readers can understand and remember key points.

- Avoid using colors in your flyer because they may not be picked up clearly in photocopies. The best contrast for readers is black print on white paper.
- Do not use black type against a dark color like red. Readers over age 40 may find such a contrast too difficult to read. If you wish to use colored paper, select a light shade so the black type will stand out.
- Use headings that emphasize key terms.
- Use bullets for short lists of pertinent topics or facts.
- Highlight date, time, and place by putting each item on its own line and centering the stacked information.

Model 5-1 announces a series of meetings in a school district. Notice that all four meetings are listed on this flyer. As the year progresses, another flyer highlighting the remaining meetings will be needed to keep attendance high.

MISSION STATEMENTS

The mission statement of a school or district is a brief description of the institution's overall academic and social goals for its students. The statement does not address specific programs or services. Although school administrators write mission statements, school boards are the official authors.

Purpose

The mission statement summarizes the school's or district's educational philosophy in terms of its values and beliefs, and the statement represents a commitment by the administration and faculty to create specific programs and services that will support the general educational goals identified in the statement. The community's question of "Where are we leading our students?" should be answered by the mission statement.

Mission statements often appear first in news releases and in the district or school newsletter. They also usually appear in the introductory materials of new or revised curriculum guides or any documents about programs of study so readers can see how the overall goals are reflected in revised coursework or learning units. Administrative long-range planning reports, grant proposals, and public relations brochures, such as those provided to real estate agents for prospective home buyers, usually contain the mission statements of the schools in the district. Official faculty and student handbooks also include the school's mission statement.

Organization

Mission statements are rarely more than half a page long. In one to three paragraphs, the writer describes the school's or district's goals for its unique student populations. Consider these questions when developing your mission statement:

- What is our school's long-range purpose?
- How do our academic and extracurricular offerings differ from those in other similar schools?
- What is our history or our special public image?
- What is our school's commitment to developing responsible citizens, lifelong learners, effective communicators, community leaders, and technologically sophisticated employees?
- Do we encourage sensitivity to diverse cultural groups?

- Do we provide opportunities for diverse cultural groups to both learn and enjoy recreational activities together?
- Do we have unique short-range goals?
- Do we have faculty and administrators with distinctive achievements that enhance our educational atmosphere?
- Do we have special technological facilities and goals?

The answers to these questions will help you develop a mission statement that reflects the unique character of your school or district. When organizing a mission statement, follow these guidelines:

Opening

- Summarize the overall goals of the school or district.
- If there is a motto that reflects the mission, include it in the opening statement.
- Emphasize that the school's mission covers educational efforts directed at all students.

Body

- State clearly that educating students and creating programs and services to meet their needs (a student-centered curriculum) is the main focus of your school.
- Include a statement about educating the whole child, stressing both cognitive and affective objectives.
- Allude to the school's reputation, history, distinctions, and awards, if relevant.
- If possible, every statement should relate to your students.

Model 5-2 shows the mission statement of an elementary school. The opening includes the school motto, emphasizes a commitment to all the students, and reminds readers of the school's long history in the community. The following sentences describe continuing adaptation of programs to student needs, the importance of all aspects of the student's growth, lifelong education, and special focus on technological growth. The closing sentence emphasizes the affective growth of students.

Although it is short, the mission statement is an important public statement about the educational commitment of administrators and faculty to the community's children.

MODEL 5–2   Mission Statement

WILLOW BEND ELEMENTARY SCHOOL
MISSION STATEMENT

The Willow Bend Elementary School has served the community for over 100 years. All members of the Willow Bend Elementary School faculty and staff believe that the school's mission is reflected in the motto "To serve all children well, in as many ways as possible."

Rigorous standards govern the student-centered curriculum, with wide-ranging programs and services. To adapt to the changing needs of our student population, curriculum is revised to reflect contemporary research and priorities. Willow Bend's commitment is to each student's growth in academics, in social relations, in good citizenship, and in preparation as a productive employee. A distinctive technology program prepares students to handle technology today and tomorrow. Students are encouraged to become lifelong learners.

All Willow Bend students must grow as unique individuals, self-confident and proud of who they are, aware of and able to develop and use their talents, abilities, and skills.

NEWSLETTERS

A classroom newsletter is usually a one-page information sheet from a teacher to parents. A school or district newsletter is usually a two- or four-page publication issued by an individual school or school district and mailed to parents, school board members, community members, business leaders, and some area superintendents.

Newsletters may appear regularly during the school year or on an occasional basis. They provide information about academic programs, special study units, behavioral rules, curricular changes, guidance activities, school and student honors, athletic achievements, general education issues, testing programs, guidelines concerning school bus safety, noteworthy school events, suggestions to parents about helping children with homework, and other issues important to the particular school or district.

Usually, administrators (superintendents and principals) organize and edit the newsletters issued by their districts or schools with the help of a faculty or staff member. Faculty, counselors, or staff members often write articles about their areas of expertise. Department chairs might offer regular articles covering course requirements and changes, department milestones (awards, recognitions of teachers, and projects), statements of goals and activities, and priorities of national subject area leaders. Students may also submit articles concerning student events, such as the Senior Class Play, the creative arts showcase, publication of the literary magazine, or the spring science fair.

Purpose

The newsletter provides information to readers interested in local education and the academic progress of students in the community. It also serves as a public relations tool. The focus in a school newsletter should be on the students' learning opportunities and extracurricular activities provided by the district or school. Always include evidence of student success in academic and extracurricular activities in your newsletter.

Readers, especially parents, want a neatly organized newsletter, carefully written and printed in clean dark type. Do not waste time and money trying to produce a slick newsletter. Too much gloss in terms of layout and print implies that outside professionals produced the newsletter, detracting from the image of building close communication between the school and community.

Also avoid sending newsletters that contain only glowing reports of students, programs, and services. Readers know about the challenging problems schools face today, and they want to see realistic reports on handling problems such as truancy, alcohol and drug use, and safety issues. Offer a balance of topics and a balanced look at how the district or school is coping with tough educational issues.

Organization

Your school newsletter, whether issued regularly or occasionally, should have a standard pattern of organization so readers become familiar with the pattern and instantly recognize features they are interested in.

Masthead.   A newsletter's title is the most recognizable feature of the first page and provides continuity for your newsletters. Some titles employ the school mascot (*Hornets' News*); others use a phrase related to the school or district (*Education Beat, District 100*); still others use the full school name to build recognition in the community (*William Clark Elementary School Newsletter*). If the school name is not in the title, include it in the masthead along with the address and telephone number.

Number each newsletter. The first year should be Volume 1, with issues Number 1, Number 2, and so on. The next year is Volume 2, with the issues starting over with Number 1, Number 2, and so on. Date each newsletter. If the newsletter does not appear regularly, you may wish to date by season (Fall 1999). Classroom newsletters may be somewhat less formal, but should be dated for easy reference.

Letter from Superintendent, Principal, or Teacher.   The first page of a school newsletter should contain a letter from the sending administrator. This letter is the most widely read item in a school newsletter because the administrator is speaking directly to the readers about the school, students, and current issues. Length may vary from issue to issue, but the letter should always maintain a pleasant tone, contain a "state of the union" message, and express interest in hearing from parents or other community members.

Model 5-3, a classroom newsletter, contains a brief letter from the teacher.

The letter from the principal in Model 5-4 establishes a cordial, optimistic tone with reminders of school goals and plans for the school year and emphasizes communication with students and parents.

Feature Articles.   The article containing the most important topic or most recent development usually appears immediately after the administrator's letter. Such topics as the school's recent reaccreditation, achievement of high ACT scores, National Merit Scholarships, athletic championships, curriculum changes, and new policies and rules are all possibilities. After the lead article, the other articles fill in the allotted space. Most business computer programs now have features that allow the user to create columns, headings in distinct typefaces, and relevant graphics. When selecting material for newsletter articles, consider the following questions:

- Is this topic newsworthy to the readers?
- Do I have enough information on this topic to write a fact-filled news article?
- What aspects of the topic appeal specifically to parents? community members? students?
- What impression should readers receive from this topic?
- Does the topic indicate a future direction for the school?
- How is the topic connected to the school's goals or mission?

MODEL 5–3   Classroom Newsletter

BRAIDWOOD ELEMENTARY SCHOOL

NEWS AND NOTES FROM THE SECOND GRADE September 4, 1999

Dear Parents and Guardians:

I am happy to have your children in my second-grade class, and I would like to introduce myself because I am new to Braidwood Elementary this year. After graduating from the University of Wisconsin in 1997, I taught for two years at Andrew Jackson Elementary School in Springdale, Tennessee, before moving here. My monthly newsletter will report on our second-grade activities, and I hope to meet all of you at our first Open House on September 28. Please call me if you have questions about your child or our learning activities. I will be glad to hear from you.

Jenny Neufeld
Jenny Neufeld

Second-Grade Screening

During September, the second graders are being screened for reading skills. This screening will help us determine how to help your child improve his or her ability to read.

Helping Flood Victims

Our second grade is joining the "Help the Flood Victims in Mexico" project by collecting canned goods. Our class voted that each student would bring one can of food on September 16. Volunteers from the Braidwood Flood Relief Committee will pick up the cans from the school collection bins. Please help your child remember this important activity by sending one can of food to school on September 16.

Meet the Police

On September 20, a police officer from the Community Police Officers' Association will visit our class and talk about how the police take care of good citizens. I think this talk will help your children understand the important job police perform in our community.

Holiday Pageant

We are thinking of having a costume parade of favorite storybook characters for our December holiday pageant. I will let you know as plans for this pageant develop.

MODEL 5–4 Middle School Newsletter

Martin Luther King Middle School Newsletter
1200 Roosevelt Parkway
Port Duncan, Maine 04689

September 1999   Vol. 6, No. 1

THE PRINCIPAL'S VIEW

Dear Parents/Guardians:

The school year is off to a good start. We have excellent participation in sports and activities, and students can anticipate many special assemblies and supplemental learning units. Creating and sustaining the strongest possible instructional program to reach each Martin Luther King Middle School student remains our commitment, fully supported by the Board of Education.

Please read this and subsequent newsletters for information about activities and programs. Our faculty and staff welcome your comments. Please call during school hours if you wish to talk to the teachers, staff, or me. With your support, Martin Luther King Middle School will continue its proud tradition as one of the finest middle schools in this region. Call our offices: 555–3495, Ext. 221, daily 8:00 a.m.–5:00 p.m.

Sincerely,

Randolph Carpenter

Randolph Carpenter, Principal

PARENTS' PERSPECTIVE

"I don't want to do that!" This particular protest often signals middle school students' rebellious independence. Guidance Counselor Melvina Gibbs reminds us that young people may experience great difficulty accepting responsibility for school requirements, home chores and errands, and participation in extracurricular activities. Guide young people toward timely completion of their responsibilities. Gibbs offers these suggestions:

- Recognize and praise jobs well done.
- Create a routine for house and yard chores.
- Post a general information list, "Things that must be done today." Provide spaces for checking off completed tasks and recording names or initials.
- Reward extra efforts with special videos, an extension of curfew, coupons, or gift certificates.

"It takes planning to encourage children's responsibilities, but it more than pays off in the long

(Continued)

MODEL 5–4 *Continued*

run," says Gibbs. "Preteens will do more than minimal effort if encouragement, praise, and rewards follow their efforts."

Melvina Gibbs can be reached daily at 555-3495, Ext. 202.

"Arnie is just not a reader—" Children follow adult models. If you have a variety of reading material at home and adults read, children want to read. Turn off the TV one evening a week. Visit local libraries regularly. Scatter high-interest material on a wide range of topics (favorite science fiction anthologies, for example) in your home. Arnie may turn into an avid reader once he's found an interesting, appealing subject.

WHAT'S HAPPENING AT MARTIN LUTHER KING?

"Sing-along Rock" Assembly October 2, 1:00 p.m.

High school musicians talk about their school's music program and lead students in singing current popular songs.

Meeting an Anthropologist October 30 (during science block)

Professor Ben Turner from Oakdale Community College discusses his career and adventures while digging artifacts in the Philippines. Slide show, fossil exhibits, and rock analysis.

Regional History November 12, 10:30 a.m.

What was this area like one hundred years ago? Local historian Bill Mox talks about early businesses and trade downtown, the railway system, high-profile residents, and ghosts and legends that survive. Exhibits.

High School Panel May 10, 1:00 p.m.

Students listen to freshmen and sophomores discuss fears and reservations about high school versus the realities.

Encourage Study Skills

Students must continue to practice good study skills now and for the rest of their academic career.

Here are some tips to help your children study.

1. Schedule quiet time for homework daily.
2. Discourage TV, tapes, radios, beepers, and telephone calls.
3. Review homework assigned; listen to your child's work plans and suggest tackling difficult assignments first.
4. Check completed assignments, encouraging perfect final copies.
5. Ask about projects related to interest areas. Students who select interesting subjects work more intensively, producing good results.
6. Review the high school handbook to preview courses and opportunities for study "down the road."
7. Encourage setting goals in each subject area, with rewards following achievement.

Feature articles follow the journalistic pattern:

Leading Paragraph

- Summarize the main points of the story. This style (called the inverted pyramid) calls for *who, what, where, when,* and *why* in the first paragraph. Even if readers skim the rest of the article, they will be aware of the main point.
- Start an article with a catchy question or quotation and then explain its relevance. "Parents' Perspective" in Model 5-4 begins with a quotation that parents will recognize.

Middle Paragraphs

- Provide details about the topic, facts, reasons for actions, anecdotes about students or events, or examples or answer questions that readers may have about the topic.
- Analyze what information will be important to readers, and focus on that.

Closing Paragraph

- Repeat a main point that you want readers to remember.
- Include a telephone number to speak to a counselor or teacher involved in the topic.
- If the topic is ongoing, promise an update in a future issue.
- Even if the topic represents a serious problem, indicate that solutions are forthcoming.

Style.   You are writing as an educator, so readers expect clear, readable news articles. In addition, follow these guidelines:

- Create an eye-catching title that also identifies the general topic of each news article.
  - *No:*   Charity Work
  - *Yes:*   Seniors Join Habitat for Humanity
- Use a conversational style with a pleasant, friendly tone. The daily newspaper strives for a neutral, objective tone, but your newsletter should project an image of approachable and concerned administrators and faculty. However, avoid slang or overly casual comments, such as "We goofed."
- Write short paragraphs. Because the text is in columns, paragraphs will seem longer than usual. Each paragraph should cover one main point.

- Write short, clear sentences, and check grammar and punctuation.
- Use bullets or numbered lists when explaining new rules or describing a series of changes, examples, or suggestions.
- Use subheadings if the article is longer than two full columns. Subheadings guide readers to specific points and help them remember information.
- Consider using a boxed section to highlight important articles or serve as a table of contents to draw readers to specific articles.
- Quote authorities or specific coaches and teachers in your article to add human interest and "put a face" on the topic.

Classroom, school, and district newsletters encourage the home–school, parent–school partnership, a key factor in students' academic achievement at all levels of learning. A regular newsletter, neatly presented and filled with relevant, well-written articles, can be a powerful tool in building community support for schools and educational goals.

POLICY STATEMENTS AND PROCEDURES

A board policy is a statement representing a school's or district's decision about a subject. The policy may reflect an educational objective, a legal regulation, a standard for behavior, or any principle that school administrators believe is essential for effective education.

Procedures are the instructions (chronological steps) or guidelines (nonchronological steps) necessary to carry out or support a policy. These are written by superintendents and school administrators. School boards sometimes review the procedures; other times the board leaves the procedures to school administrators.

Legal policies and procedures, such as those for drug searches, are usually written by superintendents and their boards. Often, outside consultants, in cooperation with state school board associations, attorneys, and other superintendents, draft policies and procedures that fulfill legal requirements and are uniform throughout the state.

School policy committees often suggest policies and procedures that cover issues related to particular schools or districts. Student handbooks contain policies related to student activities. Faculty and administrative handbooks contain policies related to professional responsibilities.

Policies

Purpose

Policies require careful thought and consideration of all factors involved. A superintendent may consult faculty, parents, community members, other administrators, and board members before being sure the policy is worded precisely. The policy should be free of ambiguous language that may create confusion or disagreement.

The policy provides a standard for consistent action in a particular school situation. Because the policy reflects a decision already made about a subject, it reduces potential conflicts among those affected by it, and it saves time by eliminating the need to rethink decisions on various school matters.

Organization

A policy statement may vary in length, but it usually is one paragraph. As a declaration of the decision about a particular matter, a policy may contain a brief rationale or background in a few introductory sentences. Specific procedures to implement the policy are written by administrators and follow the policy statement.

Not all policies, however, require procedures. The following sample policy statement does not require detailed instructions.

PARENTAL INVOLVEMENT POLICY

The Merriman School District 10 is committed to educating students with the active involvement of all parents.

POLICY: The Merriman School District 10 will identify potential barriers to parental involvement because of physical disability, economic disadvantage, limited English proficiency, limited literacy, or limited free time and will provide special opportunities so that all parents can review and evaluate school programs.

The policy has no specific procedures because administrators will handle each case individually.

Procedures

Purpose

The procedures accompanying a policy statement provide specific instruction to readers responsible for implementing the policy. The procedures may involve chronological steps in a system to be followed by one or more persons or nonchronological rules and guidelines appropriate in a specific situation. Consider your readers and their understanding of a subject so you can use the appropriate details and language. Procedures written for parents usually need more detail or definition than procedures written for teachers.

Organization

Introduce procedures with a brief statement identifying their purpose and the subject they cover. If the procedures are chronological steps, number them in the exact order in which they should be performed. Follow these guidelines:

- Explain only one step per number. If two steps should be performed simultaneously, explain the proper sequence: "When meeting a visitor in the hallway, first ask for identification, and then ask the visitor's specific destination in the building."
- Begin each step with an action verb (a command).
    1. Ask the visitor for identification.
    2. Use your beeper to alert security, if necessary.
    3. Do not try to restrain the visitor.
- Use the same terminology for a particular element throughout the procedures. Do not refer to "security monitor," "hall monitor," and "security staff" when you mean the same person.
- Use headings to help readers find specific stages of an activity.

    Before Dance
    During Dance
    After Dance

- State specific details.

    No: Write a report.
    Yes: Write a Discipline Report.

- Write complete sentences for clarity. Avoid "telegrams."

    No: Send student to ap.
    Yes: Send the student to the assistant principal's office.

- Refer readers to other steps when necessary.

    - If the substance is a prescribed medication, go to Step 16.

    Then direct readers back to a previous step or on to the next step.

    - When the prescription number is confirmed, go back to Step 12.

You may end procedures with the last numbered step, or you may conclude with a statement that reinforces the need and importance of the procedures.

If procedures are not sequential steps, use bullets to mark the individual actions. Group the actions by topic, such as "Entering the Building," or by the person responsible for the actions, such as "Counselor Responsibilities."

You may write nonsequential steps (1) in commands, (2) in the passive voice, or (3) in the indicative mood.

- Write a Discipline Report for students violating the District Controlled Substances Policy.   (command)
- A Discipline Report must be written for students violating the District Controlled Substances Policy.   (passive voice)
- The principal will write a Discipline Report for students violating the District Controlled Substances Policy.   (indicative mood)

Do not use *should* to mean *must:*

No: The counselor should inform the parent.
Yes: The counselor must inform the parent.

The word *should* could be interpreted to mean a *possible* action rather than a *required* action.

Model 5-5 shows a policy and accompanying procedures for students on school buses. The steps are not sequential and are grouped under headings that direct the reader to specific areas of discipline. The writer uses the indicative mood for sentences because the rules are directed at both the driver and the students. Commands are not appropriate because commands will not identify the person performing the action.

(See also "Instructions to School Personnel" in Chapter 3.)

PRESS RELEASES

A press release, also called a news release, is an announcement sent to the media. The press release may announce, for example, new school personnel, school policies, academic awards or athletic championships, changes in curriculum, enrollment or student testing information, new activities, and special services.

MODEL 5–5   Policy and Procedures Statement

SCHOOL BUS SAFETY POLICY: For the safety of all students who ride school buses to Centerville Middle School, transportation rules will be enforced, and violations will be addressed in a meeting with the principal, parents, and students involved.

PROCEDURES FOR SCHOOL BUS SAFETY

The following safety rules cover transportation to and from school during regular attendance hours and transportation to and from scheduled athletic events, extracurricular club activities, and field trips.

Seating

- Students must sit in assigned seating while going to and from school during regular attendance hours.

- Students must sit alphabetically beginning in the front rows from left to right when going to and from special events.

- A bus will not move from the parking area if students are standing at their seats, standing or walking in the aisles, or standing in the stairwell at the front door.

Food and Drink

- Students may not carry food or drink on the bus.

Unruly Behavior

- If students are creating excessive noise as determined by the driver, the driver will stop the bus at the nearest safe location and call the supervisor, who will inform the principal.

- Students who refuse to follow the directions of the driver will receive a disciplinary referral recommending penalty and/or immediate suspension from riding the bus.

- Students who engage in threats, inappropriate language, or practical jokes will merit a disciplinary referral and may be suspended from riding the bus for the rest of the school year.

Purpose
The purpose of a press release is both to inform the public and to create a favorable impression of the school or district. Even the announcement of an unfavorable event, such as the need to install metal detectors, should present the school as working to improve a situation or solve a problem. Because the readers of a press release are so varied, write short, clear, concise sentences and use short paragraphs.

Organization
Press releases should appear on the school letterhead and follow the standard organization and format.

Heading and Title.   The top one-third of the first page should contain the following:

- *Time of release.* Models 5-6 and 5-7 state "FOR IMMEDIATE RELEASE," the phrase used most often. You may also state a specific date, such as "FOR RELEASE MAY 22, 1999."
- *Name of a person to contact for more information.* Include the telephone number or other appropriate means of contacting the person.
- *Headline.* The headline should be short, usually no more than six words, using key words that suggest the main point of the release. Avoid catchy headlines that rely on humor or slang.

Opening Paragraph.   The first paragraph, called the lead, should contain all important information.

- Write the opening paragraph so it covers the five Ws: *who, what, where, when,* and *why.*
- Include the *how* of the situation if possible. Editors and news directors want the most important details in the lead; the release must fit the space or time they have available, and if they cut your release, they will cut from the end working backward.

Models 5-6 and 5-7 have opening paragraphs that clearly establish the subject with specific names, date, and locations. If the editor prints only the opening paragraph of each release, readers will understand the announcements although they will not get all the details.

MODEL 5–6   Press Release

RIVER FALLS COMMUNITY CONSOLIDATED SCHOOL DISTRICT
102 River Road
River Falls, IL 61440

FOR IMMEDIATE RELEASE

For More Information, Call:
Dr. Jerome R. Baldwin
(815) 555–7470

NEW PRINCIPAL FOR JAMES MONROE HIGH SCHOOL

River Falls, IL, June 29, 1998...Amanda P. Rochester has been appointed principal of James Monroe High School in Millersburg, Illinois, as of July 1, 1998. Rochester will be the first principal in the new high school building, which will open August 21 for the 1998–1999 academic year.

Rochester served as principal of Longfellow Academy, a college preparatory school, in Conway, Maine, for five years. Prior to that appointment, she was assistant principal and coordinator of the teacher-advisor program at Longfellow.

A recipient of the prestigious Windhaven Educational Grant to develop summer instructional programs for students, she says, "I believe that learning is a year-round effort." Rochester plans to introduce the summer program concept at James Monroe High School in the next few years. Most recently, Rochester has received national recognition as an "Outstanding Educator" from School Personnel magazine.

Rochester earned her B.S. and M.S. degrees at the University of Pennsylvania.

-30-

Middle Paragraphs.   The body of the press release is written in inverted pyramid style, with the most important information in the lead, followed by paragraphs containing information in descending order of importance.

- Explain the background, develop the description, and add interesting details.
- Try to anticipate questions readers may have and answer them.
- State only the facts; do not include your opinions.
- Include interesting quotations from key people, always stating their full names and titles.

MODEL 5–7   Press Release

North Division High School
1642 W. North Avenue
Tulsa, Oklahoma 74123

FOR IMMEDIATE RELEASE

For More Information Call:
Ann Ferguson
Assistant Principal
(918) 555–8993

CULTURAL DIVERSITY FESTIVAL AT NORTH DIVISION

Tulsa, OK, March 30, 1999...North Division High School will hold
a Cultural Diversity Festival for students, parents, and guests on
Friday, April 12. The all-day festival will feature speakers, group
discussion, dances, history presentations, fiction and poetry readings,
and ethnic displays. Principal Harmon Williams describes the festival
as "a day of learning about our neighbors" and an educational
experience "of great value for the future" for all students. Williams
invites members of the community to attend the events.

The festival will open with a welcome from Mayor Jones,
followed by the announcement of student essay contest winners who
wrote on "Diversity and Education." Guest speakers Raymond
Jackson, Director of the African-American Council of Oklahoma;
Suzanne Chen, Curator of the Museum of Asia in Oklahoma City; and
Jason Spencer, author of Cultural Diversity and America's Future,
will begin the day's scheduled events by sharing "ethnic turning
points" in their lives.

Festival participants will visit displays of painting, traditional
costumes, historical artifacts, and regional customs in the main
auditorium. Students representing their cultural groups will offer
insights related to the heritage of the Mexican, Puerto Rican, African-
American, Cherokee, Irish, Italian, English, and Osage people.

-more-

(Continued)

Closing Paragraph

- State general information you wish to include about the subject, such as school history.
- Include information about attending an event or state deadlines.

Notice that Model 5-6 ends with educational information about the
new principal. Model 5-7 closes with information for readers about how
to get tickets to the festival.

Closing Format. End the last page of the release with -30- or End, centered as in Model 5-6. If the release is more than one page long, all pages

MODEL 5–7 *Continued*

Participants may also tour a 32-screen video room with ongoing presentations of the historical impact of various ethnic groups. Also scheduled are ten "Myths and Legends" roundtables, where students will retell ethnic tales.

Student fiction and poetry readings will be at 10 a.m. and 12 noon in the Wilton Anders Theater, and a dance program is scheduled for 2:30 p.m. in the theater. At 4:30 p.m., "Desserts and Discussion" will allow guests to review the day's activities.

Reaching out to all community members is an objective of Mayor Jones and Principal Williams. Students will bring invitations home for parents and guests, and the day's schedule of events will appear in the <u>Community Bulletin</u> on WKXP-TV, Channel 16. Community members who are interested in attending the festival should contact Sarah Russo at 555–8993, ext. 672, to obtain passes. All those attending must have official tickets to enter the school.

-30-

---

except the last should end in -more-, centered as in Model 5-7. Place a shortened heading with the page number in the upper-right corner of all pages except the first, as in Model 5-7.

Develop a mailing list of regional papers, radio and television stations, and interested groups for your press releases. Send the release to a specific person or a particular editor, such as the education editor. (See also "Newsletters" in Chapter 5.)

Maintain Coherence in Paragraphs

Sentences must be in a logical sequence, linked by transition words, repetition of key terms, or enumeration. These elements are shown in boldface in the following paragraph:

Classes may publish home pages as part of the Sussex Country Day School web site when two areas have been considered by the teacher. **First,** teachers must check all content. **Teachers** are responsible for updating information and maintaining class-oriented content on the home **page. In addition, teachers** must ensure that the class **page** includes our school name, telephone number, and the teacher's name. Class **pages** must **also** link back to the school home **page. Second, teachers** must be very conservative in the interpretation of "fair use" of material under copyright. **For example, teachers** should assume that everything on the Internet is protected by copyright. **Under that assumption, teachers** should ask for written permission from the author of web content before using material on class home **page.**

6

Agendas and Minutes

An agenda is the official written order of business (numbered in sequence) for faculty meetings, board meetings, or any formal meeting. Minutes are the official written record of events at a meeting and record all official decisions.

AGENDAS

Agendas establish the purpose and framework for a meeting, and, if they are distributed ahead of the meeting, they allow participants to prepare for reports and discussion. Generally, the superintendent writes the agenda for a school board meeting; a principal writes the agenda for a faculty meeting; a committee chair writes the agenda for a committee meeting. Writers may solicit agenda items from participants before producing the final agenda.

Agendas may be distributed as an informal list in a memo or as a formal list. A school board meeting agenda is usually a formal list; faculty and committee meeting agendas are often announced in memos.

Formal Agendas

An agenda that follows the traditional order of business includes seven items in the following order.

- *Reading and Approval of Minutes*—Minutes are not read at the meeting if they are distributed beforehand. Any previous minutes not yet approved may be corrected and approved also.

- *Reports of Officers, Boards, and Standing Committees*—Standing committees report in the order in which they are listed in the bylaws.
- *Reports of Special Committees*—Only special committees that were instructed to report are listed.
- *Special Orders*—A special order is a particular subject that has been scheduled for a given meeting.
- *Unfinished Business*—Unfinished business covers items that have come up in previous meetings but were not completed or items that were on previous agendas but were not taken up at earlier meetings.
- *New Business*—The agenda may list items, and the chair may ask for new business from the floor.
- *Adjournment*

Agendas for board meetings, faculty meetings, and committee meetings usually reflect variations in this order or additions that suit the purpose and preferences of the participants.

School Board Meeting Agendas

A school board meeting agenda is distributed to board members, the superintendent, and scheduled speakers ahead of the meeting and to audience members at the meeting. Model 6-1 shows a school board agenda that reflects the typical business of a board meeting. Notice that items appear in short phrases without articles and coordinating conjunctions, such as item 10 in Model 6-1.

The following are typical additions to school board agendas:

- **Heading**—As Model 6-1 illustrates, school board agendas usually have headings that include the full name of the school district, the designation "regular" or "special" meeting, and the date, time, and place of the meeting.
- **Approval Items**—Introductory items usually include the approval of the agenda (or changes), approval of the minutes (and corrections), and approval of bills and payroll.
- **Welcome**—Because board meetings are open to the public, the board president generally welcomes visitors formally.
- **Reports**—Scheduled reports are listed. The chair usually asks for other reports before proceeding to the next item.
- **Educational Items/Financial Affairs/Personnel**—Board agendas often list these items by topic rather than under Unfinished

MODEL 6–1   Formal School Board Agenda

BOARD OF EDUCATION DISTRICT 56 AGENDA

Regular Meeting
Tuesday, November 30, 1999, 6:30 p.m.
Shawnee Heights High School Auditorium

1. Call to Order

2. Roll Call

3. Approval of the Agenda and/or Changes to the Agenda

4. Approval of Minutes of November 16, 1999, Special Meeting

5. Approval of Bills and Payroll

6. Welcome to Visitors

7. Reports
   "Stay in School" Teen Parent Program—Mary Roberts, MSW, Adolescent Health Care Specialist, Shawnee Heights Social Service Agency

8. Education Items
   a. Geography concepts integration, grades 4–12, Samantha Burgoyne, Chair, Geography Committee (Enc. #1)
   b. Revised math basics curriculum, grades 6–12 (Enc. #2)

9. Comments from Public

10. Financial Affairs
    a. Review of bids to resurface old gym floor, Shawnee Heights High School (Enc. #3)
    b. Review of bids for three new air conditioning units, Marshfield Elementary School (Encs. #4 and #5)
    c. Proposal for cheerleader uniforms (Enc. #6)
    d. Approve current budget items (Enc. #7)

11. Personnel
    a. Set schedule for rehiring seasonal coaches
    b. Discuss hiring two additional Forest Grove teacher aides

12. Superintendent's Report (Encs. #8 to #17)

13. New Business

14. Executive Session

15. Adjournment

Business or New Business. Topical organization helps visitors follow the discussion.

- **Comments from the Public**—Visitors, particularly parents, are usually most interested in educational matters, and the chair may call for comments at any time. Model 6-1 lists comments directly after educational items.
- **Superintendent's Report**—The superintendent's report is usually lengthy and contains information about district affairs. After the report, the chair will call for new business.

Notice that board packet materials are numbered and listed on the agenda with the relevant business item. Board members get these materials with the agenda before the meeting.

Faculty Meeting Agendas

Agendas for faculty or committee meetings are usually less formal than school board meeting agendas. Model 6-2 shows a typical faculty meeting agenda. The principal sends the agenda in a memo calling the next meeting. An agenda for a committee meeting may be a simple list of three or four items for discussion.

Although a faculty meeting may follow parliamentary procedures for motions, it tends to be less formal than a school board meeting. A formal roll call is not included, but attendance may be recorded for inclusion in the minutes. The "Announcements" section includes announcements by the principal and other announcements from the floor. In Model 6-2, the principal includes a positive comment about the successful school year, thus setting a collegial tone.

MINUTES

Minutes provide the official record of what was done at a meeting and are usually distributed shortly after the meeting. The official secretary of a group or an assigned secretary takes notes and writes the minutes, following the order of the agenda. Minutes should be a neutral record of meeting events. Personal opinions or slanted language are inappropriate. Model 6-3 shows excerpts from the minutes of the meeting announced in Model 6-1.

The following are guidelines for recording minutes of a meeting.

- State the full name of the group and the date and kind of meeting, such as regular or special.

MODEL 6–2   Informal Faculty Meeting Agenda

To: Faculty
From: Jerome Mossner   *JM*
           Principal
Date: March 20, 1999
Re: Faculty Meeting, April 12, 1999

The next faculty meeting will be on **Wednesday, April 26, 1999, at 3:30 p.m. in Room 126A.** Following is our agenda.

1. Call to Order

2. Approval of Minutes of March 6, 1999

3. Announcements

4. Reports

   Principal's Policy Committee
   Fine Arts Program Planning Committee
   Technology Workshop Committee

5. Unfinished Business

   Disciplinary Referrals

6. New Business

   Committee for May Awards Program
   Outstanding Teacher of the Year Award
   Feedback on duty assignments

7. Adjournment

Thanks to all your efforts, we have had a very successful year thus far, and I'm looking forward to a great finish. If anyone has any ideas for special recognitions for the May Awards Program, bring them up at the meeting.

- Record the names of the people present. You may also note the names of those absent.
- Note the exact time that the meeting was called to order and the name of the person presiding.
- Record approval of the agenda and any changes and approval of the previous minutes with any corrections.
- In separate paragraphs, record each item covered.
- Number the paragraphs in the minutes for easy reference.

MODEL 6–3   Excerpts from Minutes of School Board Meeting

BOARD OF EDUCATION DISTRICT 56

Minutes of Regular Meeting, Tuesday, November 30, 1999

Present: Melvin Parrington, Tracie Reese, Nathan Stern, Donald Treeter, Jon Tygum, and Superintendent Paul Porter.

1. The meeting was called to order by Board President Stern at 6:32 p.m.

2. The agenda was approved as presented.

3. The minutes of November 16, 1999, were approved with the correction that Assistant Superintendent Mark Willis was also present....

6. Board President Stern welcomed parents and community members, Shawnee Heights Music Club representative, graduate students from the School of Education, Southwestern State University, and Mary Roberts, Shawnee Heights Social Service Agency.

7. Mary Roberts reported on Shawnee Heights Social Service Agency program, "Stay in School," for teen parents. She reviewed the counseling programs and parenting classes. She and Guidance Director Mary Esparza will submit a formal written report to the board by year end....

11. Donald Treeter moved to approve the Kohls Construction low bid for resurfacing the gym floor. The motion passed unanimously....

17. Jon Tygum moved to approve a schedule for rehiring coaches and assistants at Shawnee Heights High School and Forest Grove Middle School. The motion passed unanimously....

20. There was no new business.

21. The Executive Session began at 9:00 p.m.

22. The meeting adjourned at 10:30 p.m.

Respectfully submitted,

Joel Cohen
Joel Cohen, Secretary

- Record all motions and their disposition (passed, defeated, or tabled). Include the exact wording of a motion unless it is merely to approve or reject a proposal. Record the name of the person who made the motion, but not the seconder. Record the exact vote on a motion if votes were counted. Do not include motions that were withdrawn before a vote.
- Do not record miscellaneous remarks by participants during the discussion of issues.
- Record the fact that the meeting went into a "committee of the whole," but do not record the proceedings of the committee of the whole.
- Record the fact that the meeting left the committee of the whole.
- State the exact time of adjournment. If the meeting had to adjourn because a quorum was not present, record that fact.
- Sign the minutes as the secretary.

Because minutes are the official record of a meeting and future actions may depend on decisions made at the meeting, be precise in recording motions, their resolution, votes, and other substantive matters.

Unify Paragraphs with One Main Point

Use an opening sentence to alert readers to the main point in a paragraph. The first sentence in this paragraph sets the main point; the following sentences explain it.

Please follow the established seating pattern for the convocation. Freshmen and sophomores will sit in the lower front pews. Juniors and seniors will sit in the lower rear pews and side balconies. Faculty will sit with students. Staff will occupy the back balconies. We are reserving side benches for guests. This seating pattern allows the most orderly entrance and exit.

7

Career Correspondence

The academic vita or résumé is a record of your professional accomplishments, and it demonstrates your ability to prepare a readable and organized document that provides information the reader needs. The accompanying application letter is your official request for an interview, and it is your first demonstration of your written communication skills. An employer will assume that your application letter and résumé represent the kind of work you do regularly, so your application always gets a "silent" interview as the reader considers your presentation.

ACADEMIC VITA OR RÉSUMÉ

Remember that employers receive hundreds of résumés, so yours must stand out favorably and be easy to read. Follow these general guidelines for your résumé:

- Use 8 ½ by 11 inch white bond paper, 20-pound weight. Pale cream or light beige paper is also acceptable.
- Keep 1-inch margins on all sides.
- Use a dark ribbon on your printer.
- Use boldface type or capitals to highlight sections, job titles, and activities that you want the reader to notice.
- Do not underline, box information, or list items in double columns. Many institutions now scan résumés into computer data bases. The

scanner reads left to right across the page. Double columns will create gibberish in the scanned text.

- Use strong verbs to describe your experience and activities. Action words, such as *coordinated, directed, designed, organized, recruited, supervised, prepared,* and *developed,* give the reader an image of a person who accepts responsibility and succeeds.
- Be specific and provide details. Do not write "helped coach athletes." Instead, write "coached girls' basketball team."
- Do not use personal pronouns, as in "I organized...." Begin with the action verb: "Organized...."
- Staple the pages together if your résumé is more than one page. Place your name and "page 2" on the next page and so on.
- Plan on a résumé one to two pages long if you are a new college graduate. As you accumulate experience, your résumé will become longer. Record all your career milestones. Unlike business executives, educational administrators like to see a full record of a job candidate's professional activities.

There are two basic styles of résumé: the chronological or traditional format and the functional or skills format. The chronological format is the one used most often by new graduates and people with uninterrupted career progress. List items in reverse chronological order so the reader can quickly see what you have done most recently. Models 7-1 and 7-2 show the chronological format.

The following are the major categories of information to include in your academic vita or résumé.

Heading

- List your name, address, and telephone number. If you can take calls at your present position, list both home and business addresses and telephone numbers. Graduating seniors often list both their school addresses and their home addresses.
- Do not list personal information, such as age or marital status.

Objective

- List a specific position that matches your education and experience or that repeats the job title used in an advertisement, such as "Guidance Counselor."
- Avoid vague statements, such as "a challenging opportunity." Revise your job objective to fit each position you apply for.

MODEL 7–1   Chronological Résumé of a Teacher

Kathleen S. McMillin
1434 Brook Park Road
Parma, OH 44234
(216) 555–9786

Teaching Experience

1996–present: East Division High School, Cleveland, OH
High School English Teacher, Grades 9–12

Courses Taught: English Skills I, II; English
Literature; American Literature; Advanced
Placement English

Service: Composition Committee; Curriculum
Committee; Student Activities Committee; Drama
Coach; Adviser to Creative Writing Class

1994–1996:   Cleveland Public Schools
Substitute English Teacher, Grades 7–12

1989–1993:   Robinson Athletic Club, Parma, OH
Fitness Instructor, part-time, all age levels

Education

1990–1994:   Cleveland State University, Cleveland, OH
B.A. in Education. Emphasis: English and Language
Arts, GPA 3.7 (4.0 scale)

Senior Thesis: "Writing as an Aid to Reading—A Case
Study"

Education Workshops

Summers
1995–1997:   "Teaching English in Urban Schools," Merriman
College
"Grading Practices at All Levels," Cleveland State
University
"Composition Today," Lakeland College

Certifications

25 High School Certificate, 7–12 (Language Arts)

MODEL 7–1   *Continued*

Kathleen S. McMillin   Page 2

Publications

Poetry: "A Rose Today," <u>Midwest Poetry Journal</u>, VI
                   (Summer 1997):34.
                   "Sunrise," <u>Midwest Poetry Journal</u>, V (Winter 1996):
                   9.
                   "Heat Lightning," <u>Poetry Review</u>, II (1993): 16.
                   "Kiss of Summer," <u>Cream City Review</u>, XXI (Summer
                   1995): 107.
                   "Dark Paradise," <u>Akros</u>, XXVI (Fall 1995): 87–89.

Fiction: "Legend of the Green Eyes,"<u>Destry Review</u>, VII (Fall
                   1998): 65–68, 98.
                   "Morning Song," <u>Midwest Fiction Journal</u>, XIII
                   (Spring 1997): 78–84, 112–113.
                   "The Secret of Briar Rose," <u>Women's Fiction Review</u>,
                   May 1995, 54, 97–106.
                   "Pencil Stroke," <u>Hammond Review</u>, V (1993): 12–19.

Poetry Readings

                   Women Reading Poetry, Cleveland State University,
                   April 1998
                   Jane Mitchell Poetry Festival, University of Akron,
                   September 1997
                   Ohio Regional Young Poets Festival, 1993

Activities

                   Volunteer, Greater Cleveland Community Tutoring
                       Project; Big Sisters; Songsters
Memberships

                   NCTE, SOCTE

Major Qualifications or Summary

An experienced job candidate may wish to highlight years of experience
or special training, as in Model 7-2. This section allows you to emphasize
one or two features that you want the employer to notice immediately,
such as "10 years' experience in coaching high school track" or "Nego-
tiated Teacher Union Labor Contracts."

MODEL 7–2   Chronological Résumé of an Administrator

MATTHEW W. SPENSER
5784 E. Camelot Circle
Newton Falls, IL 62434
(614) 555–3589 (home)
(614) 555–4000 (office)

JOB OBJECTIVE: Superintendent

QUALIFICATIONS: Twelve years' administrative experience
Ph.D. in Educational Administration

EDUCATION

UNIVERSITY OF ILLINOIS, Urbana-Champaign, Illinois

Ph.D. in Educational Administration, 1998. Specialized in law, finance, curriculum, and supervision.

Dissertation: "Survey of High School Principals: Communication with Parents/Guardians of At-Risk Students"
Director: J. Thomas Pakenburg

UNIVERSITY OF ILLINOIS-CHICAGO CIRCLE, Chicago, Illinois

M.S. in School Administration, 1986. Emphasis: Curriculum and Supervision
B.A. in Education, 1982. Emphasis: History and Mathematics

ADMINISTRATIVE EXPERIENCE

NEWTON FALLS CONSOLIDATED SCHOOL DISTRICT #112, Newton Falls, Illinois

Assistant Superintendent, 1996–present
Responsibilities: Staff Development, Budget Preparation, Contract Management, Program and Staff Evaluation, Curriculum, Community Relations, Community Education

Principal, Newton Falls High School, 1992–1996

MODEL 7–2   *Continued*

-2-

MOUNT WINDSOR CONSOLIDATED SCHOOLS, Mount Windsor, Indiana

Assistant Principal, Monroe High School, 1990–1992
Director, Summer School, 1987–1990
Director, Chapter One Summer Program, 1986

TEACHING EXPERIENCE

MOUNT WINDSOR CONSOLIDATED SCHOOLS, Mount Windsor, Indiana

Mathematics Teacher, Monroe High School, Grades 9–12, 1982–1990
Courses Taught: Algebra, Geometry, Calculus, Advanced Algebra

AWARDS

Illinois State School Administrator of the Year, 1996
    "Implementation of Belt-Tightening Budgets for Schools"
Teacher of the Year, Mount Windsor Consolidated Schools, 1989
Illinois Board of Regents Scholarship, 1978–1982

PROFESSIONAL SEMINARS ATTENDED

Collective Bargaining Seminar, Roosevelt University, 1996
Seminar on School Law for Principals, Roosevelt University, 1995
Illinois Principals' Academy, Purdue University, 1994

PROFESSIONAL MEMBERSHIPS

Member, Illinois Association of School Administrators
Member, Illinois Principals' Association

SPEECHES AND PRESENTATIONS

"Contract Management: A Win-Win Opportunity," National School
    Administrators Convention, 1998
"Communication with Noncertified Staff," School Personnel
    Conference, 1997
"School-Community Relations," Newton Falls Chamber of
    Commerce,1995
Panel, "Evaluation Instruments, A Review," Illinois School Board
    Convention, 1995

CERTIFICATION

Illinois Superintendent Certificate
Illinois and Indiana Principal Certificates
09 Teaching 6–12, History, Mathematics

Education

This category is next on the résumé if you are a new college graduate without significant work experience.

- List your education in reverse chronological order, your most recent degree first.
- Omit high school.
- Include all four-year and two-year colleges and list special certificates you earned or professional seminars you attended.
- State the full name of the program and full name of the school. Include the city if it is not in the school name.
- List your grade-point average if it is high and indicate the scale (3.7 GPA on a 4-point scale).
- If you prefer, list only your grade-point average in your major (3.7 GPA in major).
- Include any academic honors or awards in this section after the school entries, or list multiple honors in a separate section later in the résumé.

Experience

This category follows "Education" if you are a new graduate, but if you have significant experience in your field, put this section ahead of "Education."

- List your teaching or administrative experience in reverse chronological order.
- Include practice teaching.
- State the full name of the school and city or province.
- State the dates of employment, such as "1990–1993" or "Summer 1994." Do not list days or months.
- If you have had the same seasonal job for several years, list the position once with the appropriate dates, such as "Summers 1989–1994: Tutoring in Project Catch-Up, Longfellow Elementary School."
- Describe your responsibilities for each job you list, particularly for those jobs related to the position you are seeking.
- If a job is unrelated to your current career goals and the title is self-explanatory, such as "sales representative," you do not need to describe your responsibilities.
- List the courses you taught under each position and any committee work, coaching, or advising.
- Identify any teaching or educational experience in jobs not connected to schools, such as "Trained managers in motivation techniques."

- List several positions at one school or district under the full name of the school or district in reverse chronological order, as in Model 7-2.

Military Experience
- List military experience separately, if it is extensive, or list it under "Experience."
- Include your rank, unit, where you served, and any command experience.

Honors and Awards
- List scholarships, prizes, and awards received in college or from professional and community activities.
- List academic honors, such as "magna cum laude."

Professional Activities
- List professional activities, such as conference committees and memberships in professional associations or civic groups.
- List any offices you have held, such as "Treasurer, 1990–1992," or special organizing functions you performed, such as "Organized Community Bond Support Group, 1995").
- List any professional presentations and publications. If you have a significant number of publications or presentations, list them separately.
- Do not list high school activities after you get a college degree.
- Do not list college activities after several years on the job.

Certification
Include all certifications that are current. These may be in the education section or separately.

References
Do not list references on the résumé. Some people prefer "References available on request" as the last line of a résumé; others omit the statement. Be prepared to offer references when asked.

Model 7-1 is the résumé of an experienced teacher. Under "Experience," she lists courses taught and all committee and extracurricular work. She also lists the professional workshops she has attended as part of the state requirement in continuing education for all teachers. Her "Education" section includes the title of her senior thesis—an expected entry on a teaching résumé. The thesis also supports her teaching interests. She has published poems and short stories and lists those individually with full information about the journals, dates, and page numbers. She also lists her appearances at poetry readings because they reflect her experience in public speaking. The other activities listed all reflect her professional interests.

Model 7-2 is the résumé of an experienced administrator who is seeking a position as a superintendent. He begins his résumé with "Education" because his Ph.D. is just completed, and he wants it to stand out on his résumé. He lists the title and director of his dissertation. His present position as assistant superintendent is the usual but not exclusive path to a superintendency, so he lists his responsibilities to emphasize his preparation for the executive position. He includes professional seminars focused on administrative matters, and he lists speeches and papers he has given at professional conferences. He also lists his certifications for administrative positions and teaching.

Your résumé should reflect your professional credentials and emphasize the items you believe are especially relevant to the position you want.

APPLICATION LETTER

One of the most important messages you will ever write is an application letter for the position you want. The application letter highlights the credentials you believe are most important for a particular position and requests an interview. The letter also demonstrates your written communication skills. Write your application letter after preparing your résumé, so you can focus the letter on key items in your résumé. Model 7-3 is an application letter that would accompany the résumé in Model 7-1.

When writing your application letter, follow these general guidelines:

- Use the same paper that you use for your résumé.
- Follow the letter format guidelines in Chapter 2.
- Address the letter to a specific person if at all possible.
- Never mail your résumé without an application letter attached.
- Do not staple the letter to the résumé.
- Mention specific details in your letter, such as school names, dates, and programs, even though these details also appear in your résumé.
- Restrict your letter to one page unless you are applying for an executive position, for which readers expect longer letters.

MODEL 7–3   Application Letter

1232 Chester Blvd.
Cleveland, OH 44241
February 6, 1999

Mr. Charles S. Ashland
Superintendent
Mount Vernon Consolidated School District #80
1000 Pine Tree Road
Mount Vernon, Mississippi 38799

Dear Mr. Ashland:

I am applying for a position as a high school English teacher in your district. Although I am presently a tenured teacher at East Division High School in Cleveland, I wish to relocate to your area to be near my aging parents in Leesburg, who require my assistance.

As you can see from my résumé, I have over five years' experience in teaching English and composition in high school. Because of my interest in creative writing, I organized a creative writing club in 1996. The club has grown from six interested students to a group of twenty-seven eager writers. In 1998, two of the students placed in the top 25 of the state poetry writing competition.

In addition to my B.A. in education from Cleveland State University, I have attended six professional workshops on current educational issues. I believe these workshops have strengthened my ability to handle the challenges in today's classroom.

I will be visiting my parents March 8–12, and I would appreciate an opportunity to talk to you about my credentials and the possibility of teaching in your district. I usually can be reached any day after 4:30 p.m. at (216) 555–9786. I have voice mail for messages.

Sincerely,

Kathleen S. McMillin

Kathleen S. McMillin

- Do not say anything negative about yourself. Change "I do not have much experience in..." to "My experience has been primarily in...."
- Concentrate on what you can do for the institution, not what it can do for you. Avoid saying, "Teaching at Madison High School would be good experience." Write instead, "I believe my special training in teaching at-risk students would be helpful at Madison High School."

Although you may send your résumé to dozens of institutions or school districts, tailor your application letter to the specific position and institution. The application letter has three distinct parts.

Opening
- Identify the name or type of position you are seeking.
- Identify where you saw the position announcement and the date.
- Identify the person who recommended that you apply.
- Explain why you are applying to this district or institution. In Model 7-3, the writer begins by stating her interest in a position in that district and explains why she wishes to relocate to that area.
- Mention at least one of your major qualifications for the position. In Model 7-3, the writer explains that she is a tenured teacher in Cleveland, thus stressing her experience.

Body
The body of your letter may contain one or more paragraphs. In this section, draw the reader's attention to the specific experience, education, and activities that make you qualified for the position. Do not rely on the reader to find the important items on your résumé. In Model 7-3, the writer discusses her teaching experience and describes the success she has had in developing a student creative writing group. She is showing the reader how her personal interest in writing supports her activity as a teacher. In another paragraph, she points out her attendance at professional workshops that focus on current educational issues. You do not have to discuss your credentials in the same order in which they appear in your résumé.

- State specifically what your degree is and where you studied if you are a new graduate.
- Mention any advanced degrees and your specialty.
- Mention any further training, such as professional seminars.
- State specifically where you are teaching or working as an administrator currently.

- Mention specific accomplishments or significant activities, such as curriculum development.
- Explain any coaching experience.
- Explain any significant research, such as surveys, testing, or classroom studies.
- Mention any extraordinary administrative experience, such as labor negotiation, community–school outreach, or program development.
- Mention any significant awards in teaching, research, or administration.
- Mention any significant community leadership, such as directing a charity drive.
- Mention any leadership positions in professional organizations.

The writer in Model 7-3 uses separate paragraphs for her teaching experience and her educational background. Do not overload one paragraph with multiple accomplishments. Group them by topic.

Closing
- Ask specifically for an interview.
- Mention times and days that are convenient for you, but also state that you will come for an interview at the employer's convenience. Because the writer in Model 7-3 is seeking a position in another part of the country, she asks for an interview during the week she will be in the area.
- Provide a telephone number and a time when you can be reached easily.
- Reaffirm your interest in the position or the district.

Write Concise Sentences

Omit superfluous words and unnecessary repetition.

No: In the month of June, we will have the final results of our survey of student activities. There may be reason, based on the results of the study, to discuss and consider limiting extracurricular activities and groups.

Yes: In June, we expect the results of our survey of student extracurricular activities. We then may consider limiting such activities.

8

Oral Presentations

Although educators are used to presenting course material and presiding over classroom discussions, formal speaking in front of parents, community leaders, other educators, and peers often creates anxiety.

The purpose of most oral presentations to adult audiences is to explain local educational issues and programs, describe the status of educational issues, offer suggestions for handling school issues and activities, or report studies and research about educational topics. Oral presentations have some advantages over written documents.

- The speaker can get immediate audience feedback and answer questions about data on the spot.
- The speaker's personality can create enthusiasm and instill confidence in the audience.
- The speaker can emphasize one of several topics, which might be covered equally in a written report.
- Listeners can raise new issues on the spot, giving the speaker new ideas.

Oral presentations also have some disadvantages over written documents.

- Listeners can be easily distracted by outside noises, audience unrest, room conditions, and their personal concerns.
- Spoken words disappear, and listeners remember only a portion of what was said.

- Time limitations require speakers to condense and omit material, possibly eliminating important details.
- Listeners have difficulty following complicated information, especially financial data.
- Listeners may be influenced by others in the audience and agree with those opposed to the speaker's message.

The key to successful oral presentations is to consider your audience, their need for information, and your purpose in communicating with them, just as you do for written documents.

PREPARATION AND DELIVERY

Much of the anxiety over giving an oral presentation can be reduced by adequate preparation.

Organization

Organize oral presentations as carefully as you do a written report. Do not rely on your memory to put topics in an effective order and report complicated data. Do not mark up a copy of a written report for an oral presentation because you will have to fumble with pages as you speak.

Prepare a key word or sentence outline of your presentation. If you are especially nervous about speaking, a sentence outline offers more supporting detail as you speak. Type outlines on regular-sized paper with at least four lines between items or on note cards with one or two topics per card. Prepare handouts or visual aids for important financial or numerical information. Plan on three basic sections in your presentation:

Introduction

- Establish the central subject of your talk.
- Explain the importance of this subject to this audience. Remember that parents have a different perspective on an issue than school board members do. You may have to define terms for one group and not for another. One group may need an introduction to the major elements of a subject; another group will not.
- State whether you want to take questions as you go along or at the end of the your talk. Taking questions as you go along may create time problems and significantly interrupt your presentation. Holding the question and answer session until after your talk is usually best.

Main Topics

- Include specific examples to reinforce your points.
- Number items for the audience as you talk so listeners can know where one point ends and another begins.
- Focus on the relevance of the information to this audience.
- Refer to other schools with the same issues; cite relevant government regulations; quote authorities.

Conclusion

- Summarize the main points you want the audience to remember.
- Remind the audience about any expected future actions.
- If persuasion is your main purpose, repeat the major benefits expected from your proposed action.

Delivery

Your delivery techniques will strengthen or weaken the impact of your talk. Thorough preparation is the first step to controlling nerves and creating rapport with the audience. Consider these guidelines for effective delivery:

- Rehearse your talk aloud so you are comfortable with the material and it fits the allotted time.
- Check the pronunciation of names or unusual terms ahead of time.
- Speak at a normal pace. Nervous speakers sometimes race through a talk in a monotone or pause after every few words, creating a stop–start pace.
- Dress conservatively. Classroom or coaching attire may be too casual for speaking to parents, community groups, or school boards. Standard business attire will usually be appropriate.
- Establish good eye contact, and give the impression that you are speaking to all the individuals in the room. Do not focus on only one or two individuals or gaze around the room without focusing on anyone.
- Avoid nervous mannerisms, such as fiddling with glasses, jewelry, clothing or note cards. Do not make artificial gestures. If you feel clumsy, keep your hands still or rest them on the lectern.
- Learn how to use the visual equipment before you begin. If the equipment breaks down during your talk, simply continue without it. Trying to fix it will distract the audience, and you may never fully regain their attention.

Question and Answer Session

In the question and answer session following your talk, answer as many questions as your time permits. If someone asks a question you cannot answer, say so and promise to find the answer. If someone asks about confidential information, explain that you are unable to reply because of confidentiality. If you are not sure what a questioner is asking, rephrase the question by saying, "Are you asking if…?" Keep calm; never resort to sarcasm or heated disagreement.

SPEAKING TO COMMUNITY GROUPS

Educators often have to speak to community groups about issues facing the local schools, and the group members usually have diverse opinions and interests in the subject. Audience members also may have conflicting and inaccurate information about a subject. When preparing your presentation for a community group, consider these guidelines:

- Use a prepared outline of key items you wish to cover.
- Indicate that you are there to clarify issues and provide facts.
- Invite questions about rumors.
- Avoid a nonchalant or seemingly lighthearted view of school issues.
- Indicate when you are speaking for the school board and when you are explaining government directives or regulations.
- If many people wish to ask questions, limit the number of questions per person or the amount of time per person.
- Present a positive outlook, emphasizing school success or potential benefits for student learning.
- If your topic involves numbers, use a visual aid to illustrate. Pie charts and bar graphs are easy to understand illustrations.
- Acknowledge negative information, but emphasize how the school or district is handling the situation.

SPEAKING TO PARENTS

Parents have the most personal and intense interest in school affairs. Their children's education and well-being are directly related to school programs, discipline, safety, and extracurricular activities. Consider these guidelines for speaking to parents:

- Recognize that school issues often evoke strong emotion in parents.
- Use the opportunity to interpret district priorities, legal requirements, state and federal mandates, and research about teaching methods.
- Relate all issues to the goal of providing a superior educational environment for their children.
- In dealing with negative information, focus on solutions.
- Stress the parents' role in their children's education.
- Offer suggestions for actions parents can take to enhance their children's learning opportunities.
- Relate board issues to specific school situations.
- If appropriate, provide a handout illustrating financial information; a list of key administrators and telephone numbers; dates of school board meetings; and names of advisory committees and task forces. Include deadlines for action.
- Urge participation in appropriate committees and projects.

SPEAKING TO SCHOOL BOARDS

Superintendents make regular reports to school boards, but boards may also request special presentations from the superintendent, teachers, counselors, and committees or task forces. Consider these guidelines when speaking to a school board:

- Acknowledge the board members' interest in all facets of district educational efforts.
- Explain any relevant district background that recently elected board members may not know.
- Emphasize facts, figures, state and federal regulations, costs, practicality, school and district policies, established procedures, legal ramifications, and actions in other districts.
- Offer handouts with detailed numerical data in tables and graphs.
- Explain relevant research and its relation to local school matters.
- If appropriate, provide a variety of perspectives, using students, teachers, coaches, and counselors as speakers for five-minute segments.
- Recommend specific actions, including timetables, budgets, and procedures.

SPEAKING TO CONVENTIONS

Educators are speaking to their peers at professional conventions. The audience is interested in exchanging information and ideas about school issues. Each participant expects to come away with practical, economical, and tested suggestions for dealing with school problems or supporting educational programs. Every convention has participants who are attending for the first time and who want to meet others in their fields. Always carry business cards with your business telephone number, address, and e-mail address. Follow these guidelines when speaking to a convention audience:

- Prepare a handout for those attending your session. The handout might be an abstract of your talk, a copy of the full talk, excerpts, or graphics showing important statistics or comparisons. Always include your name, address, telephone number, and e-mail address on the handout.
- Prepare visuals (overhead transparencies, video tapes, or slides) to illustrate your main points or statistical information as you speak.
- Observe the time limitation carefully. Presenters become angry when their time is limited because another speaker has taken too much time.
- Use realistic examples in your presentation. Relate issues to how your school or district handled them. Paraphrase student or teacher response to events or activities.
- If there is no established question and answer time, plan on reserving at least five minutes of your time to answer questions.

SPEAKING AT AN ACADEMIC CONFERENCE

An academic conference emphasizes research studies and attracts educators with advanced degrees. Participants want to hear about new research, either completed or in progress. Often an academic conference includes individual research papers, panel discussions of trends in educational theory, and poster presentations that briefly introduce research projects. Most of the presentations represent work in progress, and speakers may be testing a research theory on an audience of peers in order to elicit feedback and suggestions.

Educators attending academic conferences usually spend a significant amount of time networking to learn about professional association activities, hiring in higher education, and publication opportunities. Academic conferences have a limited number of sessions, and program committees are highly selective. Whether you are presenting an individual research paper, giving a poster session, or participating in a panel discussion, consider these guidelines:

- Pay close attention to your time limits to avoid infringing on another presenter's time.
- Read a prepared paper if that is the usual format for the conference. Practice reading the paper to be sure that it fits into the time allotted. Usually, speakers allot two minutes per page for a read paper.
- Speak from a detailed outline if that is the usual format for the conference. Do not attempt to present research information from brief notes or from memory.
- Prepare visual illustrations of key points, or prepare a handout with the key points, especially when numbers are involved.
- Prepare a one-page abstract of your talk as a handout.
- Bring several copies of your full paper for those who want one, or offer to send copies to those who want one.
- Put your name, school address, telephone number, and e-mail address on every handout.
- Carry business cards with you for those who ask.
- If you are giving a poster presentation in a large room with other presenters, prepare a five-minute summary of your project because people tend to move on to other presenters after that length of time.
- For poster presentations, prepare a lengthy abstract as a handout for those who stop at your table.
- Prepare an illustration of two or three key concepts for a poster presentation. Some people prepare large heavy board posters; others prepare smaller cardboard posters that are easier to pack.
- If you are on a panel, be prepared to adjust your remarks depending on what others may say. If the person speaking directly before you states some statistics that you had intended to give, indicate that those statistics are important, but do not repeat the numbers verbatim.

The more oral presentations you do, the more relaxed and confident you will be about selecting relevant information for the audience.

Avoid Overloading Sentences

Short sentences are easier to read and understand than long, complicated sentences.

No: For the Bank-at-School Program, we will have teacher manuals with lesson plans on economics, banking practices, credit, savings, and loans; a bank representative will visit our school monthly to accept deposits and counsel students about banking procedures and their plans for savings, helping students understand financial skills through one-on-one explanations.

Yes: For the Bank-at-School Program, we will have teacher manuals and monthly visits by a bank representative. The manuals contain daily lesson plans for understanding economics, banking practices, credit, savings, and loans. The bank representative will accept deposits and counsel students about banking procedures and their plans for savings. The bank representative also will help students learn financial skills through one-on-one explanations.

9

Grammar

Every revision process must include a check of grammar. The following items cover the most troubling questions.

AGREEMENT

Agreement refers to the correct form necessary when parts of a sentence must correspond in terms of gender, number, or person. A pronoun, therefore, must agree with its antecedent, and a verb must agree with its subject.

Pronoun Agreement

A pronoun must agree in gender, number, and person with the noun or pronoun to which it refers:

No: Each teacher must record attendance on their master list.
(The noun *teacher* is singular, and the pronoun *their* is plural.)

Yes: Each teacher must record attendance on his or her master list.

Yes: All teachers must record attendance on their master lists.

No: After hearing the student's excuses, I did not believe it.
(The noun *excuses* is plural, and the pronoun *it* is singular.)

Yes: After hearing the student's excuses, I did not believe him.

Yes: After hearing the student's excuses, I did not believe them.

No: The School Board met at their usual site.
        (*School Board* is singular and requires an *it*.)
Yes: The School Board met at its usual site.

Subject–Verb Agreement

The verb in a sentence must agree with its subject in person and number.

No: The report of the Joint Commission on Secondary Schools suggests that more needs to be done to keep students from dropping out.
        (The subject is *report* and requires a singular verb.)
Yes: The report of the Joint Commission on Secondary Schools suggests that more needs to be done to keep students from dropping out.
No: The high number of students who failed were disturbing.
        (The subject is *number* and requires a singular verb.)
Yes: The high number of students who failed was disturbing.
No: Frank and Jeff swims with the Houghton Swim Club.
        (Two or more subjects joined by *and* require a plural verb.)
Yes: Frank and Jeff swim with the Houghton Swim Club.
No: Either Barbara or Jane are responsible.
        (Singular subjects joined by *or, nor* require a singular verb.)
Yes: Either Barbara or Jane is responsible.
No: Neither coaches nor teachers is invited to the meeting.
        (Plural subjects joined by *or, nor* require a plural verb.)
Yes: Neither coaches nor teachers are invited to the meeting.
No: Several minor squabbles or one major fight seem to occur every Friday afternoon.
        (When one subject is plural and one subject is singular, the verb usually agrees with the nearest subject.)
Yes: Several minor squabbles or one major fight seems to occur every Friday afternoon.

MODIFIERS

Modifiers are words, phrases, or clauses that describe or limit other elements in the sentence.

Dangling Modifiers

All verbal phrases, prepositional phrases, or dependent clauses must refer to a subject in the sentences. *Dangling modifiers* do not refer to a subject in the sentence. They occur most often at the beginning of a sentence, but they may also occur at the end. Rewrite the sentence to include the subject of the modifier.

> *No:* Realizing the problem, procedures for safe fire drills were distributed.
> (The participial phrase *realizing the problem* does not refer to the subject *procedures*.)

> *Yes:* Realizing the problem, the assistant principal distributed procedures for safe fire drills.

> *Yes:* The assistant principal realized the problem and distributed procedures for safe fire drills.

> *No:* To go on the field trip, parent permission forms must be turned in.
> (The infinitive phrase *to go on a field trip* does not refer to the subject *forms*.)

> *Yes:* To go on the field trip, students must turn in parent permission forms.

> *Yes:* Students who want to go on the field trip must turn in parent permission forms.

> *No:* Worried about his grades, a teacher conference was necessary.
> (The participial phrase *worried about his grades* does not refer to the subject *conference*.)

> *Yes:* Worried about his grades, the student requested a teacher conference.

> *Yes:* Worried about his son's grades, the parent requested a teacher conference.

Misplaced Modifiers

Words, phrases, or clauses that do not refer logically to the nearest word in the sentence are *misplaced modifiers*. Rewrite the sentence to place the modifier next to the word to which it refers.

> *No:* The teachers presented test results to the school board that showed increased student achievement.

(*Student achievement* refers to the *test results* not to the school board.)

Yes: The teachers presented test results that showed increased student achievement to the school board.

Be especially careful about placing single-word modifiers directly before the words they modify:

- The memo said that *only* teachers were invited upstairs.
- The memo said that teachers were invited *only* upstairs.
- The memo said *only* that teachers were invited upstairs.

In these three examples, the placement of the word *only* changes the meaning of the sentence. The first example restricts who was invited; the second example restricts where teachers could go; the third example restricts the memo content.

Squinting Modifiers

Words or phrases that could logically refer to a preceding word or a following word are called *squinting modifiers.* Rewrite by moving the modifier.

No: The band members promised in August to learn several new marches.
(The phrase *in August* could refer to when the promise was made or when the band would learn the marches.)

Yes: In August, the band members promised to learn several new marches.

Yes: The band members promised to learn several new marches in · August.

PRONOUN REFERENCE

Pronouns must refer clearly to one specific antecedent in the sentence. If necessary for clarity, repeat the specific term instead of using a pronoun.

No: Barbara and Erica decorated the gym, but she put up the crepe paper alone.
(The pronoun *she* could refer to either woman.)

Yes: Barbara and Erica decorated the gym, but Barbara put up the crepe paper alone.

No: Plans call for a new parking lot, a new outdoor track, and completely renovated gym locker areas. It will add $100,000 to the cost.
(The pronoun *it* does not clearly refer to one item.)

Yes: Plans call for a new parking lot, a new outdoor track, and completely renovated gym locker areas. The improved locker areas will add $100,000 to the cost.

No: The Booster Club, Big Sisters, and Homecoming Leaders will be at the rally. They will introduce two new cheers.
(The pronoun *they* does not clearly refer to one group.)

Yes: The Booster Club, Big Sisters, and Homecoming Leaders will be at the rally. The Big Sisters will introduce two new cheers.

No: Teachers checked off names and told them to form lines before boarding the buses.
(The *names* could not form lines.)

Yes: Teachers checked off names and told students to form lines before boarding the buses.

SENTENCE STRUCTURE

Readers need clear sentences. Avoid the following serious faults in sentence structure.

Comma Splice

A *comma splice* (sometimes called a *comma fault*) occurs when the writer joins two independent clauses with a comma. Rewrite by (1) creating two separate sentences, (2) adding a coordinating conjunction (*and, but, or, nor, for, so, yet*), (3) placing a semicolon between the two independent clauses, or (4) making one of the clauses dependent.

No: The graduation proficiency tests should be easy, however, teachers will offer students after-school tutoring for two weeks before the test date.
(The conjunctive adverb *however* cannot link two sentences.)

Yes: The graduation proficiency tests should be easy. However, teachers will offer students after-school tutoring for two weeks before the test date.

Yes: The graduation proficiency tests should be easy, but teachers will offer students after-school tutoring for two weeks before the test date.

Yes: The graduation proficiency tests should be easy; however, teachers will offer students after-school tutoring for two weeks before the test date.

Yes: Although the graduation proficiency tests should be easy, teachers will offer after-school tutoring for two weeks before the test date.

Fused Sentence

A *fused sentence* (sometimes called a *run-on sentence*) occurs when a writer combines two or more sentences without any punctuation between them. Rewrite by creating independent sentences or place a semicolon between the sentences.

No: School counselors are planning to present a "Dressing for Job Interviews" session for seniors most seniors will attend the Saturday program.

Yes: School counselors are planning to present a "Dressing for Job Interviews" session for seniors. Most seniors will attend the Saturday program.

Yes: School counselors are planning to present a "Dressing for Job Interviews" session for seniors; most seniors will attend the Saturday program.

Hidden Fragment

A *hidden fragment* is an incomplete sentence because it does not have a subject or a verb or both. These hidden fragments sometimes occur when the writer begins a sentence with the relative pronouns *who, which,* or *that* or begins a sentence with a very long introductory phrase. Rewrite by creating a full sentence or combining the hidden fragment with another sentence.

No: The football coach gives pep talks to the players before each game. Which creates team spirit.

Yes: The football coach gives pep talks to the players before each game. The talks create team spirit.

No: Referring to the school board report that reviewed the need for capital funds for the next decade.

Yes: Referring to the school board report that reviewed the need for capital funds for the next decade, the principal requested a new cost study.

No: The bus driver filed a written report about problems with students on the bus. Students being very boisterous and putting their heads out the windows.

Yes: The bus driver filed a written report about problems with students on the bus. Students were very boisterous and put their heads out the windows.

No: Ron Wilson's home run won the game for us. The game that cinched the title for Wellman High.

Yes: Ron Wilson's home run won the game for us. This game cinched the title for Wellman High.

Write Sentences in Active Voice

Write sentences with the subject performing the action.

No: The report will be written by the principal.

Yes: The principal will write the report.

No: The student will be counseled.

Yes: Ms. Perkins will counsel the student.

10

Punctuation

Because you are an educator, your writing will be looked at with an especially critical eye. Your revision process must include a check of punctuation. The following is a brief guide to the punctuation marks that are most often troubling.

APOSTROPHE

An apostrophe shows possession. For singular nouns, add an apostrophe followed by an *s*; for plural nouns ending in *s*, add only the apostrophe. If the singular noun ends in a multiple *s* sound, add only the apostrophe.

- The teacher's analysis of the records showed problems in students' attendance patterns.
- The seventh-grade girls' folders were missing from the district's main office.
- The report on the Williames' children was incomplete.

The apostrophe also marks the omission of letters in a word or in dates.

- The results of the school board election weren't known until the next morning.
- The funding continued through the '90s.

Do not confuse *its* (possessive) with *it's* (contraction of *it is*).

- Because it's raining, we can't have the rally on the playground.
- Professor Truxall is studying the high school's academic program and its changes over time.

COLON

The colon introduces lists or explanatory phrases or clauses. A complete sentence, or independent clause, must precede the colon. Do not place a colon directly after a verb.

- The assistant principal asked for three reports: weekly attendance figures, total budget and breakdown for fall sports, and evaluative reports from department chairs.
- Mr. Billings reported finding inadequate security procedures, decreased hallway monitoring, and high absenteeism.

COMMA

The comma has numerous uses. The following are the most common:

To link—The comma links two independent clauses joined by a coordinating conjunction (*and, but, or, for, so, yet* and *nor*).
- The principal stopped the fight, but students were in an uproar.
- Ms. Smith directed the school play, and Ms. Perkins led the school band.

To enclose—The comma encloses parenthetical information, simple definitions, and any expressions that interrupt the sentence.
- Miranda Gillam, principal of Koslow High School, was named Whittier County Educator of the Year.
- Excessive absence, ten or more days, requires a parent/guardian and principal conference before a student may reenter school.
- The teachers, of course, deserve the credit for overall excellent student scores on the Woodward Eighth-Grade Skill Assessment Test battery.

If the phrase or clause is essential to the meaning of the sentence, do not enclose it in commas.

- Principal Fuller honored the students who were in the 90th percentile of the Challenge Curriculum Program. (The phrase *who were in the 90th percentile* is essential in identifying which students were honored. Such phrases should not be set off by commas.)

To separate—The comma separates introductory phrases or clauses from the rest of the sentence.

- Although he had never been on a track team, Michael Tibbs ran the 50-yard dash in his physical education class and amazed instructors.
- Because so many students were sick with the flu, the Alamo History program was postponed.
- To coordinate our extracurricular efforts, I need a report of activities from each teacher.

Commas also separate items in a list. Most stylists believe that the comma should appear before the final *and* in a list to help readers recognize the final item.

- Teachers ordered chalk, overhead transparencies, audio tapes, and masking tape.

Commas also separate items in dates and addresses.

- Year's End Test Score Reports, dated June 15, 1999, were sent to Kurt Meek, Superintendent, Monmouth County District Office, 235 Sunset Drive, Adams, IL 60019.

DASH

The dash (typed as a double hyphen with no space before or after or as an em dash) encloses phrases or words that interrupt a sentence and also sets off words or phrases at the end of a sentence. The dash can also enclose simple definitions within a sentence. The dash is an especially emphatic mark of punctuation and increases the focus on the words that follow it or that are enclosed.

- The team has only one problem—no uniforms.
- The majority of female students—those who took the test in October—passed.

Do not overuse the dash as a general substitute for a comma.

EXCLAMATION POINT

The exclamation point indicates strong emotions or sharp commands. Used with commands, it creates a harsh, dictatorial tone, and readers usually resent both it and the writer. Most writing does not require an exclamation point, but, used sparingly, it may be effective in newsletter articles or announcements that indicate happy surprise.

- South Central's basketball team won the Southeast Valley Conference Regional Championship!
- Our student service groups raised more money for the homeless than did groups at any other high school!

HYPHEN

The hyphen divides a word at the end of a typed line and also forms compound words. Modifiers of two or three words before a noun require hyphens.

- Due to a computer-technology mishap, we must reregister all transfer students.
- Our Adult-Back-to-School program is off to a great start.
- We need up-to-date laboratory equipment.

Hyphen use tends to change over time. *Today* was once *to-day.* If you are in doubt about whether to use a hyphen or how to divide a word, consult a recent dictionary.

PARENTHESES

Parentheses enclose nonessential information or simple definitions within a sentence and numbers or letters that enumerate items in a list.

- Colton Sherwood (a 1996 graduate) spoke at the Homecoming Weekend Rally.
- The secretary will prepare (1) parent name tags, (2) faculty name tags, (3) a floor plan with faculty names and room numbers, and (4) a survey form for parents.

- The Board of Education unanimously passed a Service Learning Requirement (student volunteer work in the community) at its meeting on April 13, 1999.

(See also "Brackets" in Chapter 11.)

QUOTATION MARKS

Quotation marks enclose (1) direct quotations and (2) titles of newspaper or magazine articles, conference papers, reports, songs, poems, and individual episodes of radio or television programs.

- Principal Hernandez opened the program by saying, "I welcome you all to our new auditorium."
- The keynote address was "How to Bring Our Schools into the Next Century."
- Does anyone have a copy of the article "Students and Extracurricular Activities"?

Place commas and periods inside the quotation marks. Place colons and semicolons outside the quotation marks. Place a question mark inside the quotation marks if the quotation is a question. If the quotation is not a question, but is included in a question, place the question mark outside the quotation marks. (See also "Italics" in Chapter 11.)

SEMICOLON

The semicolon links two independent clauses without a coordinating conjunction (*and, but, or, for, so, yet,* and *nor*).

- The principal suggested holding pep rallies in the auditorium; the coach preferred to have the rallies on the practice field.
- All the children are registered; however, we may have more transfer students by Monday.

The semicolon also separates items in a series if the items contain internal commas.

- Assigned to the Governor's Committee for Secondary Education were Geneva Dobbins, Principal, Kennedy High School, Trail City; Howard Redwing, Director, Montana Educational Research Institute, Mission Ridge; and Robert Harrod, Director, Association for Educational Perspectives, Jefferson City.

SLASH

The slash separates parts of dates, addresses, and numbers and may indicate choices.

- For more information, call 555–8786/8899. (choice of two telephone numbers).
- Testing began on 9/23/98 with ⅔ of the female students and ½ of the male students.

(See also "Mechanics" in Chapter 11.)

Maintain Conventional Usage

Do not substitute **being** for **because.**

No: Being that the pep rally is scheduled at 3 p.m., we will postpone the faculty meeting.

Yes: Because the pep rally is scheduled for 3 p.m., we will postpone the faculty meeting.

Do not substitute **myself** for **I** or **me.**

No: The principal invited Ms. Jones and myself to participate.

Yes: The principal invited Ms. Jones and me to participate.

No: Ms. Jones and myself gave the presentation.

Yes: Ms. Jones and I gave the presentation.

Do not confuse **imply** (to suggest) with **infer** (to assume or draw a conclusion).

The principal's remarks **implied** that the hall monitors were not supervised. Teachers **inferred** that he wanted them to check monitors every period.

11

Mechanics

When you are revising a document, double-check the mechanical details of writing.

ACRONYMS AND INITIALISMS

An *acronym* is an abbreviation formed from the first letters of the words in a name or phrase. The acronym is written in all capitals with no periods and is pronounced as a word.

- The official name of Indiana's state exam, required for public high school sophomores, is the ISTEP Plus (Indiana Statewide Testing for Educational Progress Plus Graduation Exam).
- In 1996, the Council of Chief State School Officers, under the direction of Dr. Scott Thomson, Executive Secretary of the National Policy Board for Educational Administration, created ISLLC (Interstate School Leaders Licensure Consortium).

An *initialism* is also an abbreviation formed from the first letters of words in a name or phrase. In an initialism, each letter is pronounced separately. Some initialisms are written in all capitals; some are written in capitals and lowercase letters. Some are written with periods; some are not. If you are uncertain about the correct form of an initialism, consult a recent dictionary.

- The C.P.A. conducted the financial audit in the district offices and sent a preliminary report to the IRS office.
- A letter from the Willard School Parent–Teacher Organization (PTO) to all Willard faculty and staff invited them to a fall luncheon during the first staff development day.

When using acronyms or initialisms, spell out the full term the first time it appears in your text and place the acronym or initialism in parentheses immediately following it to be sure readers understand the meaning. If you are certain your readers know the acronym or initialism very well, you can use it without stating the full term first. Plurals of acronyms and initialisms are formed by adding an *s* without an apostrophe, such as YMCAs, M.A.s, IEPs, PTAs, ACTs, and SATs.

BRACKETS

Brackets enclose words or phrases that are inserted into quotations by writers or editors. The inserted words are intended to add information or clarify the original quotation.

- Superintendent Johnson opened the two-day conference by saying, "We are all thankful for the splendid service by Coordinator Lucinda Matlin [1976–1998] and her outstanding contributions [photographs from each conference] to the archives."

Brackets also enclose a phrase or word inserted into a quotation as a substitute for a longer, more complicated phrase or to clarify.

- "The new curriculum focuses more attention on [self-directed learning] and allows more teacher interaction with students who need closer supervision," commented the assistant principal.

(See also "Parentheses" in Chapter 10.)

CAPITAL LETTERS

Capital letters mark the first word of a sentence and the first word of a quotation. A full sentence after a colon and a full sentence in a numbered list may begin with a capital letter if the writer wishes.

- The teacher entered the classroom, smiled, and said, "Hello, welcome back to school."
- Many high school teachers want increased security in the hallways: Checks at all entrances are essential.

Capital letters also mark the proper names of people, places, and objects.

Dr. Monica J. Wilkinson
Ford Taurus
The Crystal Palace in London

Capital letters mark (1) religions, (2) nationalities, (3) tribal affiliations, (4) linguistic groups, (5) geographical areas, (6) organizations, (7) events, (8) historical periods, (9) software, and (10) calendar designations.

Greek Orthodox (religion)
French (nationality)
Apache (tribal affiliation)
Celtic (linguistic group)
Great Plains (geographic area)
American Association of School Administrators (organization)
Superbowl (event)
Renaissance (historical period)
Windows 97 (software)
Wednesday, May 29 (calendar designation)

Capital letters mark brand names, but not generic names.

Tylenol (acetaminophen)

Capital letters mark the first, last, and main words in the titles of (1) books, (2) articles, (3) reports, (4) films, (5) television and radio programs, (6) music, and (7) art works.

Realm of the Incas (book)
"Profile of Maria Gomez, Teacher of the Year" (article)
"Study of Test Results for Grades 4 and 5" (report)
Strangers on a Train (film)
Ancient Mysteries (television program)
"White Christmas" (music)
Waterloo Bridge, Gray Day (art work)

Many institutions also use capital letters in specific circumstances not covered in grammar handbooks. If your institution requires a specific style for certain words or terms, follow that style.

ELLIPSIS

An *ellipsis* (three spaced periods) indicates an omission of one or more words within a quotation. When the omission is at the end of the quotation or includes an intervening sentence, the ellipsis follows the final period.

- The keynote speaker stated, "Let us all pledge now...to support rigorous standards for our children...."

ITALICS

Italics set off or emphasize words and phrases. If italic type is not available, underline the words or phrases. Italics set off titles of (1) books, (2) periodicals, (3) plays, films, television, and radio programs, (4) long musical works, (5) complete art objects, and (6) ships, planes, trains, and spacecraft. The Bible and its books are not italicized.

House of Glass (book)
Cleveland Plain Dealer (newspaper)
Oklahoma (play)
The Gold Rush (film)
Masterpiece Theater (television program)
Rigoletto (long musical work)
The Thinker (complete art object)
Titanic (ship)

Italics also set off words discussed as words and words or phrases in a foreign language or Latin. Scientific terms for plants and animals are also italicized.

- The term *distance learning* refers to video presentations or programs, lectures, and activities that originate in facilities outside the students' immediate educational setting but that may involve interactive exchanges between presenters and students.

- The biology class gathered nuts from the nearby hickory trees (genus *Carya*) for closer study.

(See also "Quotation Marks" in Chapter 10.)

LISTS

Lists highlight information and guide readers to specific facts, tips, or instructions. Items in a list should represent similar content. If the list covers items that need to be purchased, do not include an item that needs to be repaired. If the list covers actions that need to be completed, do not include a nonaction. The following list represents a grouping that is not similar in content:

- new band uniforms
- 6 new computers
- broken front door lock
- loose handrail at front entrance
- missing board in back hall step
- 12 liquid boards with erasers

This list should be separated into two lists:

Items that we need to have in the next budget:

- new band uniforms
- 6 new computers
- 12 liquid boards with erasers

Items that we must repair:

- back hall step—missing board
- front door lock—broken
- front entrance handrail—loose

Lists must also be parallel grammatically. Do not mix nouns, sentences, infinitive phrases, and other forms. The following list is not grammatically parallel:

We have the following costs:

- Postage is $75 per mailing to parents.
- Telephone—$389
- Using the fax machine—$67
- To print newsletters—$134 per month

Rewrite the list to achieve parallel structure in each item.

We have the following costs:

- Postage—$75 per mailing to parents
- Telephone—$389
- Fax machine—$67
- Newsletter printing—$134 per month

Lists with numbered items imply either that items are in descending order of importance or that items are numbered sequentially. This list, implying sequence, is from a principal's memo to the faculty:

Please conduct the following identification check in your homeroom on Friday morning:

1. Identify students who have no ID.
2. Enter their names on the attached ID Identification Sheet.
3. Ask students without IDs to fill out the attached forms.

Lists often do not imply sequence or importance. In that case, use bullets to mark the listed items. *Bullets* are small, black circles that appear in place of a number. The following list is from a memo to faculty:

Please be sure to turn in the following before October 1:

- Academic progress reports
- Attendance reports for students absent more than five times
- Requests for spring field trips

MEASUREMENTS

Measurements of physical quantities, sizes, and temperatures are expressed in figures. Use abbreviations for measurements when you are also using figures if you know that your readers can understand the abbreviations. Do not use periods with measurement abbreviations unless the abbreviation might be confused with a full word; for example, *inch*, abbreviated *in*, needs a period to avoid confusion with the word *in*. Use a hyphen when a measurement functions as a compound adjective before a noun. Do not use abbreviations if no numbers are involved.

- The teacher used 6-in. pipes in the experiment.
- The cooking demonstrator served pudding in 2-oz cups.
- Several pounds of dirt were dumped in the hallway.

If the measurement involves two numbers, spell out the first or the shorter word.

- The architect suggested three 12-ft high pillars in the central hallway.

NUMBERS

Use figures for all numbers over ten. If a document contains many numbers, use figures for all numbers so readers will not overlook them.

- The building custodian reported 16 brooms, 3 dustpans, and 5 sets of gloves missing from the storeroom.

Do not begin a sentence with a figure. Rewrite to place the number later in the sentence or spell out the number.

No: 26 teachers attended the conference.
Yes: Twenty-six teachers attended the conference.
Yes: The conference attracted 26 teachers.

Use figures and words for very large numbers that would be hard to read if written out.

6.4 billion people
$27 million

Use figures for references to (1) money, (2) temperatures, (3) decimals and fractions, (4) percentages, (5) addresses, and (6) book divisions.

$43.78
70°
7.50 and 7 ½
15%
635 N. 129th Street
Chapter 6, page 104

Use figures for the times of day. Many people get confused over A.M. and P.M. in connection with 12 o'clock. Indicate noon or midnight in parentheses to clarify the time.

6:35 P.M.
12:00 (noon)

To make numbers plural, add an *s* without an apostrophe.

3s   1990s   12s   504s

SYMBOLS

Symbols should appear in parenthetical statistical information, but not in the narrative.

Incorrect: The *M* were 4.58 for Test 22Y.

Correct: The means were 4.58 for Test 22Y.

Incorrect: The sample (number = 455) was selected from high school juniors.

Correct: The sample (N = 455) was selected from high school juniors.

Formulas or equations that require handwritten symbols should always be set off on a separate line to ensure clarity.

(See also "Punctuation" in Chapter 10.)

Eliminate Trite Language

Try to avoid using expressions that may once have been fresh but have been overused for years.

Examples: It has come to my attention
                   last but not least
                   at this point in time
                   put our shoulders to the wheel

Index of Models

Subject Index